12/19/73

camilo torres

his life

and his message

The text of his original platform
and all his messages
to the Colombian people

edited by John Alvarez Garcia
and Christian Restrepo Calle
translated by Virginia M. O'Grady

TEMPLEGATE PUBLISHERS
SPRINGFIELD, ILLINOIS

translated by Virginia M. O'Grady from
Camilo Torres: *Biografia-Plataforma-Mensajes*
published by Ediciones Carpel-Antorcha,
Medellin, Colombia

manufactured in the United States of America
Library of Congress Catalog Card 68-28866

a
preface

by dorothy day

How impossible a thing Christianity is, so deep a wound to man. Non-violence as a mass movement to bring about social change began only with Gandhi. Christianity is two thousand years old, and a thousand years are as one day. We are, in effect, only two days old, and infantile in our knowledge of God and His ways with men, His willingness to transform man, to divinize him, to make man partaker of the divine life, capable of overcoming evil with good and of transcending the sufferings of the time and the martyrdoms that will come about in the attempt to work for "the new heaven and a new earth wherein justice dwelleth."

Meanwhile, the command to love our brother means to know him, to study his condition, here at home among the Blacks, in Latin America among those who are a new people—by blood, Indian, Spanish, Negro, Portuguese but now Mexican, Colombian, Brazilian—certainly a beginning of brotherhood that we in the United States have not yet dreamed of as coming about in the future.

How many Negroes or Indians do we know among the millions that live among us in ghettos, on the land, or in the city? In how many of their homes have we lived, slept in their beds, eaten with them at their tables? And how many have been our guests, sharing with us what we have? Do we know each other at all? One could say that we have not come so far as the Latin American, as he is termed, in achieving brotherhood, in combatting racial discrimination.

Simon Bolivar's victory in 1824 ended more than 300 years of Spanish domination in the New World. There is a dream among Latin American students today that there will be another liberation brought about by a coalition of not only all the progressive political parties, students and peasants, but of all the countries of Latin America. Perhaps it is the fear of this which has brought about the presence of our United States Army Green Berets in Latin America, those military advisors whose purpose is to train army troops to combat the guerrillas.

During the Third World Congress of the Laity, held in Rome in October, 1967, representative speakers from Latin America pointed out that the guerrilla movement was present in almost every country and was not to be minimized.

Colombia was the first area of the American continent visited by the Spanish explorers. The Dominicans accompanied the first settlements, and a bishopric was established in 1514. Fray Juan de

Queveda, Fray Domingo de las Casas, and St. Louis Bertrand were famous early Dominicans. The Jesuits came later and founded in 1572 the oldest college in America still directed by its founders. St. Peter Claver, apostle to the Negro, was the most famous of the Jesuits there.

Colombia covers an area four times the size of the state of Arizona. The population in 1938 was roughly nine million and now in 1968 it has more than doubled to nearly nineteen million. It is a country of mountain ranges and great rivers. Bogota, its principal city, lies at an altitude of 8,650 feet above sea level. There are 160,000 Aborigines in the eastern plains and river basins, and also civilized Indians who retain their own language and culture. There are nearly one hundred native languages spoken. The population is 35 per cent pure white, five per cent Negro, two per cent pure Indian and 58 per cent mixed. There are vast tracts of land not under cultivation and great areas still unexplored. Half the people depend on agriculture and twenty-four families, it is said, rule the economy which is over-dependent on coffee production. There has been some land distribution, but the land owners failed to implement the reform laws, and the cost of living rose 20 per cent in 1965.

The economic situation of Colombia today was analyzed in an article in the *Commonweal* by Alexander W. Wilde, a student of Latin American affairs who has lived for some time in Colombia. "As much as 30 per cent to 40 per cent of the population of Colombia's mushrooming cities live in the sub-proletarian slums around them. Twenty per cent of the urban work force is unemployed. Of the 150,000 entering the labor market each year, only about 12,000 will find jobs." And yet the poor keep coming to the city to catch the crumbs falling from the tables of the rich, enticed by the glitter, and the stories of the higher salaries of those who do succeed in getting jobs in industry or in service.

"Sixty-one per cent of Colombia's agricultural land belongs to 3.6 per cent of all land owners, and 4.6 per cent of the population receives 40.6 per cent of the national income. Its infant mortality rate is ten per cent, and it has the highest birth rate in the hemisphere. There are 2.5 doctors for every 10,000 people. Each year 25,000 children die of malnutrition. Illiteracy is above 40 per cent and only eight per cent of Colombians receive an education beyond the primary level."

It was into this upper four per cent of the population that Camilo Torres was born in February, 1929. He first attended a German school in Bogota which was closed in 1941. Camilo's father had been consul to Berlin in the early thirties.

I heard the details of Father Torres' life from his brother, Dr. Fernando Torres, neurologist at the University Hospital in Minneapolis, Minnesota, from his wife, Gertrude, an Austrian woman raised in Switzerland, and from his young son Mauricio, who is majoring in political science at Macalester College in St. Paul.

The Torres family have been in Minneapolis for some time, and I was having dinner with them in their beautiful home on Mt. Curve Avenue. They have several Colombian servants with them, and the place seemed more like an embassy than a doctor's home. And indeed I found later that Dr. Torres is Colombian consul in Minneapolis. Many young Colombians have been getting their higher education at the University of Minnesota, where Dr. Torres also lectures. Camilo Torres had also taken courses and lectured at the University when he visited Minnesota on two occasions.

Their mother is a militant woman, much interested in politics, and I heard from Mrs. Fernando Torres the story of a demonstration in which the mother had led a few thousand women through the streets of Bogota. The demonstration had been broken up by the police with streams of water from fire hoses.

Young Camilo continued his studies, after the German school in Bogota had been closed, at a Catholic school where he studied law.

"At this time," Dr. Torres went on with the story of his brother's education, "he was not leading at all a good life. He was running around with a wild set, and had no interest whatever in religon. We did not think much of the Dominicans who were his teachers, but later some French Dominicans visited, and perhaps it was then that Camilo became interested in a group of young people who were devout, and especially in a young girl. He was very much in love with her, but she entered the convent and so there was no question of marriage. It was not long after that that he announced that he wanted to be a priest, and that he was going to join the Dominicans."

"His mother was furious," Gertrude Torres continued the story. "She is a very strong woman. She would take to arms herself in political trouble. She went right after him and dragged him home by force."

I pictured to my mind a matriarch, and when I was shown pictures of the tall slim woman—she is still living in Bogota—I could well see how she could overcome her impulsive son. She did agree, however, to his attending the diocesan seminary. When Camilo proceeded to Louvain, there was some opposition to his going to what was considered a hot bed of revolution.

"They called it a Communist university," Mrs. Torres put in. "But he went, sponsored by the Cardinal, and took his advanced studies there."

During vacations he drove by Volkswagen through Eastern Europe, Czechoslovakia, Poland and East Germany, as well as through France, Italy and Spain.

In addition to studying the writings of Teilhard de Chardin, Jacques Maritain and the works of Abbe Pierre (these are all mentioned by his friends) Torres also studied Marxism in books and in action in Eastern Europe. He must have known, too, of the worker priests and the writings about those initiators of social action.

When he returned to Colombia, after his first visit to Minnesota, he lectured in the National University and later also worked as chaplain there. He was not content to lecture on social change but began to train his students to join with peasants and workers in a communal effort to attack the problems of the slums, this huge area on the outskirts of Bogota.

Land which was formerly used only for grazing cattle was given to the Indians. He taught them. He started a pilot farm and founded schools. The authorities accused him of organizing a Communist camp for the training of guerrillas. He wanted to train shoe-makers, tailors, and to establish a medical clinic. It was on one of his two visits to Minnesota—one was to be with his father who was undergoing surgery—that he tried (with the aid of Father Garrelts, who was president of the Newman Club, and also his confessor while he was in the United States) to get shoe-making machinery as a small industry for his pilot project in Colombia.

Controversy with Cardinal Concha over his political activities led him to ask for laicization. This was granted in June, 1965. He continued his public life of trying to unite students and peasants and city workers into one party, traveling and speaking through the country, but finally he became convinced that he must identify even more with the people for whom he had worked since he began his research as a university student, and he joined a guerrilla group. News of his death came a few months later. On February 15, 1966 it was learned that Father Camilo Torres had been shot to death by government forces in the course of a skirmish with a guerrilla band that he had been leading. He was thirty-seven years old at the time of his death.

Father Torres never abandoned his priesthood. In his message to the Communists and his message to the Christians, both of which were printed in the Havana periodical, *Bohemia,* on January 21, 1966, he wrote that his course was dictated by his conscience, and that when there was a just social order established in Colombia, he would return to his priesthood.

"At first, I wished to return to my country to help her because of my love for Camilo Torres," his nephew Mauricio said to me. "But now it is for love of my country first, then my love for him."

"When I returned to my country after the death of my brother," Dr. Fernando Torres told me, "I wrote to the newspapers that I did not wish to make the death of my brother, at the hand of government forces, the occasion for the streets of Bogota to flow with the blood of my own people."

Dr. Torres' letter was printed in all the Bogota newspapers and it did indeed prevent the violence which was about to erupt in the seething population.

"We do not want our Colombians to make a god of him either," Mauricio said.

The name of Father Torres has been in the news many times this month of February, 1968. According to the Religious News Service, in the Argentine where there is a military government, there is a great deal of underground activity which involves both priests and religious laymen. One group calls itself the "Camilo Torres Commandos." In Brazil,

Bishop Jorge Marcos de Oliveira of Santo Andre, stated publicly that he would not oppose a popular armed revolution, and that he thought that Pope Paul would also support such a revolt. In November a group of 300 priests sent a collective letter to the hierarchy of the country protesting the unjust social structure; a national budget which allots more to armed forces than to social welfare, health and education; and paternalism and lack of dialogue in the Church. The construction of expensive church buildings while the poor went hungry was also criticized. In Peru, Cardinal Landazuri Ricketts refused to approve of the building of a basilica in honor of the patron saint of Peru, St. Rose of Lima. He said that the money should be used to set up educational and health facilities in the slums.

And now in both England and America, with their own racial conflict, the story of Camilo Torres, who is considered a martyr by his peers, has influenced the beginning of what can be termed a "theology of violence."

In England, the New Left magazine *Slant* commented in an editorial in the April-May, 1966, issue: "It is too easy for intellectuals to opt for leadership as opposed to the real struggle. In a very real sense Torres was the embodiment of what *Slant* stands for, the working out of a Christian mission in terms of a revolutionary community of belief. Christian action now is precisely what Torres did in Colombia; that is, a direct involvement in the international struggle."

Stories about Father Torres appeared in the *Commonweal,* in *Ramparts,* and in *Liberation* in the United States, and the press of many other countries carried feature stories about him.

Che Guevara in a message to the "Executive Secretariat of the Organization of the Solidarity of the People of Africa, Asia and Latin America" written from South America—his last communication with the Cuban people—calls attention to Father Torres' death in Colombia a few months after the priest had given up his teaching post at the University of Bogota and joined the guerrillas. This appeared in April, 1967, in a special supplement of *Tricontinental,* a news magazine in Havana.

In the *Journal* of the Moscow Patriarchate, October, 1967, there is an article by Archpriest P. Sokolovsky, *Christianity and Revolution.*

"Local Catholic leaders," he writes, "are inclined to consider not only the revolutionary transformation, but the very word revolution as something obviously communist, deserving excommunication. Due to this, it is understandable why certain prominent Catholic priests who seek to sacrifice themselves for the struggle, take off their cassocks, proving by their very act the purity of their priesthood. 'I have taken off my cassock in order to be a truer priest,' the Colombian priest theologian Camilo Torres told his friends. At times only such an act can incite the directors of the churches to change their attitude to the revolution and to those who fight for it. The life of Father Torres convinces us of this. In his struggle he remained a Catholic and a priest and was in the common front with the Marxists."

The Third World does not consist of the two great Communist powers and the Western powers which have grown rich in the last century. It is the world of South America, Asia and Africa. It also exists wherever there are still classes and races which are oppressed, and we cannot help but think of our own country with its rural poor and its Mexicans, Puerto Ricans and Blacks, as the Negro—the Afro-American—now prefers to be called.

"An irresistible urge is working these poorer elements towards their betterment by liberating them from all oppressive forces," sixteen bishops write in *New Blackfriars,* December, 1967. And they go on to speak of revolution. "The Church is not wedded to any system, least of all to the international imperialism of money and today the social doctrine of the Church, reaffirmed at Vatican II, is already dissociating her from this imperialism of money, one of the forces to which she has been for a time tied. She is not wedded to any system any more than she once was to the monarchy and feudalism of the *ancien regime,* any more than she will be in the future to some form of socialism. . . . Nevertheless, throughout her long pilgrimage on earth the Church is *in practice* always tied to the political, social and economic system that in a given period, ensures the common good, or at least an ordered society. . . .

"Taking into account certain necessities for assuring material progress, the Church has for a cen-

15

tury tolerated capitalism with its legalization of lending at interest and other practices that so little conform to the moral teaching of the prophets and the Gospels.

"She cannot but rejoice to see another social system appearing that is less far from that teaching. . . . Christians have the duty to demonstrate 'that true socialism is a full Christian life that involves a just sharing of goods, and fundamental equality.' (Patriarch Maximos IV at the Council, 1965) Far from sulking about it, let us embrace it gladly, as a form of social life better adapted to our times, more in keeping with the spirit of the Gospel. In this way we shall stop people confusing God and religion with the oppressors of the poor and the workers, which is what the feudal, capitalist and imperialist systems are. . . .

"The Church greets with joy and pride a new mankind that respects not money concentrated in a few hands, but the workers, the laborers and the peasants."

In an article about the Peasant Republics in Colombia, published in October, 1965, in *Monthly Review* (New York), Father Torres, accused of being a half-Communist priest, is quoted as testifying at the National Congress of Sociology held at Bogota in 1963.

"The administration of justice," he said, "is beginning to be practiced among the guerrillas and even within those groups of peasants who were victims of official persecution. The informal rules and sanctions were military and administrative, ways of controlling the peasant population in general and the groups of combatants in particular. The so-called peasant republics to which official authority has no access, developed here in Colombia. And an administration parallel to the official one was organized within them, with new responsibilities and functions. The recently organized peasant groups not only exert pressure on this informal administration, but we are aware of how the presence of guerrilla groups has a decisive influence on the administration of justice and the replacement of judicial functionaries. Likewise we know that many others have to respect the opinions of the great regional leaders in charge of the combatant groups. . . . The guerrillas have imposed the discipline demanded by the peasants themselves; they have rendered authority more democratic; and they have given trust and security to our rural communities. We mentioned this when discussing the feeling of inferiority which has disappeared from the peasant areas where the phenomenon of violence has been manifested. All these socio-cultural changes in the peasantry have transformed it into a pressure group demanding a general modification of structures. . . .

"In spite of everything, violence has released a social process unforeseen by the ruling classes. It has awakened the peasant's consciousness; it has given him group solidarity, a feeling of superiority and sureness in action; it has opened up possibilities for social improvement and it has institutionalized his aggressivness, with the result that Colombian peasants begin to prefer the interests of the peasantry to that of the party. This will have as an effect the constitution of a socio-economic and political pressure group capable of producing structural change in the way least foreseen and desired by the ruling class. We can say that 'the violence' has constituted for Colombia the most important socio-cultural change in the peasant areas since the Spanish conquest."

In November, 1965, this same New York magazine states, "The Colombian Father Camilo Torres is not a guerrilla, but he is strongly influenced by the guerrilla activity throughout the country. Despite the fact that he has been accused of being a 'half-Communist priest' he has openly indicated his difference with the Communist Party by proclaiming a program far to the left of the Party's, a program which ties him to the leftist revolutionary groups and sectors of his country."

The Colombian "peasant republics," whose existence though fluid is none the less real, number almost a dozen. It was estimated that about 7,000 peasant families live in Marquetalia. According to *Monthly Review*, the army in 1964 launched an offensive against six of these little republics: Rio Chiquito, El Pato, Guayabero, Sumapaz, Tequendama, and Marquetalia. If they are "fluid" they must certainly continue to exist.

Legends and news spread among the peasants in mountain and jungle—legends filled with humor. One story is of the fantastic escapes—how one guerrilla leader turned himself into a bunch of bananas or a little dog.

"There we were shooting into this cabin," one army sergeant told an imprisoned revolutionist: "It's impossible to nab that Yon Sosa. Just imagine, once we had him surrounded, him and all his group, in a house. There was a gun battle which lasted an hour. Suddenly, he and his men stopped shooting. We waited. Silence. About an hour passed. Then the door opened and a little black dog trotted out. You won't believe me but it was Sosa himself, escaping us disguised as a dog." (Quoted from *Monthly Review*, May 1965, p. 20.)

The same article tells of an evangelist travelling through the mountains with a Bible and reading to the peasants the stories of the Maccabees, telling them to fight for justice too. There are stories of insurrection throughout the Bible.

Yes, there were the Galileans, known for their readiness to revolt against Roman rule, and many another group among the Jews in the days of St. Paul, which lead, according to Abbe Fouard, to Paul's famous words of *Romans 13* about authority —such bitter gall to the revolutionist, and to the pacifist too who uses the non-violent means of civil disobedience.

It is understandable that men like the priest Camilo Torres should take arms, that men like the Maryknoll priests, Fathers Thomas and Arthur Melville, should have followed his example. But another Maryknoll priest has undergone the crucifixion of being taken from his work in Guatemala and sent elsewhere. He has chosen obedience as the better part. (The motto of Pope John XXIII was

19

'Obedience and Peace.') He is a priest, and to paraphrase the words of Job about the God who afflicts him, "Though He slay me, yet will I trust in Him."

This morning as I sat in church waiting for Mass to begin, I was still thinking of Camilo Torres and the ideas for which he had died. Earlier on that morning I had read over again that thrilling manifesto entitled *Gospel and Revolution,* signed by those sixteen bishops of the Third World, issued sometime early last year, published in French in *Temoignage Chretien* on August 31, 1967 and translated into English and printed in *New Blackfriars,* Cambridge, England.

In the same issue there is a review of the book, *The Grave of God,* by Father Robert Adolphs. The reviewer says that Father Adolphs is not just joining the popular 'Death of God' game. "He takes his starting point at the person of Jesus—where else is there for a Christian to start from?—and the emptying He undertook 'taking the form of a servant.' The Church cannot be greater than her master. It is not renewal that will serve today but *Kenosis,* emptying."

I began to think of the outward Church, the respectable Church, and the accusation that it is not relevant today. I began to think of all the people I knew who had fallen away from church-going, from the Sacraments. Certainly over the decades I had met people, dedicated people, finding their religion in service, in union activities, in teaching, in emptying themselves. And in revolution.

Revolution has followed revolution in Latin

American countries, but new revolutions have emerged which are unlike any other we have seen.

Camilo Torres joined the guerrillas, their life in mountain and jungle, joined their pilgrimage to the people, the campesinos. He broke bread with them, and so truly became the *companero,* the one who breaks bread, the companion.

What would Mass be like in a jungle, in one of the encampments of the republics in Colombia where no priest had been sent as missionary, where the idea of the Church was linked up in the minds of the destitute with the rich, the exploiter?

Suppose a priest like Father Torres looked at his companions sitting around a fire by night, hunted men, but men bringing a gospel of hope to the poor, men who were workers themselves, unlearned men like the twelve apostles. Suppose he picked up bread —in this case tortillas—and after speaking to them of the first communion at the Last Supper, and using the gospel words, broke and gave it to them. Suppose he had wine, as the fugitive priest did in Graham Greene's book *The Power and the Glory.* And suppose he blessed the cup and passed it to them all, for the forgiveness of sin. Would not this be a church, there in the wilderness? Would not this be a Mass? Would not this community of men have communion together just as the two men walking with Christ on the way to Emmaus did, as they sat at the inn and knew Him in the breaking of bread? And could it not be just as casual and as quiet, and yet just as earthshaking?

You will say, "How can they go unless they are

21

sent? And who will send them?" Christ sent the apostles, and the apostles sent others, and so it has come down all along the centuries, despite the hundreds of heresies and schisms, despite the corruption of the Church, where "charity had grown cold" at even so early a time as that of the beloved apostle John.

Who will send them? What bishops will send them? Such bishops as these sixteen who have written such a manifesto. Missionaries such as the Maryknoll fathers are "guests," they have said, in the country where they sincerely go to serve. Guests of whom? Of the oligarchy which also welcomes the exploiters of the people who come to invest money, developing the resources of the country and then taking more money out? Or are they guests of the Church in that country, of the bishops there? Could they not presume permission until they could reach the bishops who are with the poor, and who would grant it? Red tape, bureaucracy are ever present and sometimes it is hard to wait when men are living on the brink of death, and ready to lay down their lives for their brothers. "Greater love than this no man hath."

News accounts are always conflicting. Priests like the Fathers Melville, recently expelled from Guatemala, suspended by their superiors and now returning to help the guerrillas, have said that they would never bear arms, nor would they take life.

What will they do then, when they have "emptied" themselves and have gone to join the enemies of the rich? What have they to give, when they have emptied themselves of the material resources of the missionary society?

This is but a meditation, resulting from my familiarity with the atmosphere of revolution. I traveled the length of Cuba five years ago from Havana to Santiago de Cuba, and I talked not to the leaders of the new socialist government but to the children in the plaza, to the school boys, to the bus drivers, three on each bus on the long trip from Havana to Santiago; when they spelled each other, they came back and sat with me because I was a foreigner and they were curious and because I had a transistor radio (a good one which I had picked up in a pawn shop on the Bowery just before I left for Cuba). I talked with hotel clerks, with shopkeepers, with the doctors in the hospital and pupils in the school named for Camilo Cienfuegos and the school teachers in Manzanillo, and with the fishermen on a dock in Bayarmo, with priests and sisters at the shrine of Our Lady of Copper outside of Santiago, with an old priest in Santa Clara, with the Johnsons, two American teachers there. I visited a granja, a collective farm, with Mrs. Marjorie Rios and her daughter, and met the people they had "alphabetized"—it was the year of alphabetization. I visited a private holding nearby (one can own up to sixty acres) and was served tiny cups of coffee in a grass-roofed hut, and the sons looking like western cowboys came in from their fields and laughed as they pointed to the Chinese oil lamp hanging from the rafter in the primitive living room. It had not been lit, they said, for evening

lessons since Marjorie Rios came there months before. I would like to go back again and see how the
granja is making out and to visit others of these
state farms where there is work the year round and
decent housing and a bit of land for all, and co-
operative stores and meeting halls. Two members
of the Little Brothers of Jesus live and work in one
of them. In Havana I stayed with Teresita and
Eduardo Casas, both of whom had finished their
schooling in New Rochelle and Fordham, and with
Lou and Lenna Jones who worked in the Department of Education.

It is the example of Cuba and its continuing
revolution that has inspired other Latin American
countries. It is the example of Sandino in Nicaragua who was pursued as a guerrilla leader in the
later twenties and for whose cause I worked when
I was still studying to become a Catholic. My job
then was doing publicity for the Anti-Imperialist
League, an affiliate of the Communists in New
York. It was in doing such work that one studied
the history of a country, and one wondered what
the United States Marines were doing in Nicaragua, and whose interests they were protecting,
just as I wonder today at United States officers
training troops in Guatemala, Bolivia, Nicaragua,
and doubtless other Latin American republics.

One story I heard in Cuba was that of a member
of Fidel Castro's original group of guerrillas who
said the rosary daily during the campaign, and
after the victory in 1959, he was assigned by Fidel
Castro to head the work in the big mental hospital

24

outside Havana. I tried to meet him while I was there, but he was away; but I saw the new buildings that were being put up and I heard, too, that a chapel would be part of each of the smaller pavilions. But this may be legend.

Father Sardinia, a Cuban priest who has since died, bore arms during the early days, and urged the priests to stay in Cuba rather than leave the country. Father Biain, Franciscan, a Basque priest, wrote a weekly story, often running into two columns, for *El Mundo,* giving the epistle or gospel of each Sunday, besides a homily. He brought news of other priests coming into Cuba from Canada, Belgium and Spain to supply the lack. The churches in all the cities I visited were open and I was able to get to Communion each day. There were no chapels in the Cuban schools, nor any in the countryside. It was the Catholic schools which were confiscated, the schools which, it was charged, were for the rich and which taught counter-revolution and awaited and hoped for the invasion of United States troops to retake the property of American corporations which had been expropriated.

Father Don Hessler, a Maryknoll priest, had invited me to come to Mexico City on my roundabout way home from that visit to Cuba, to speak to the Catholic Family Movement. My talk was not well received. No offers of hospitality came from any of the families and Father Hessler had to put me up in a little hotel. The Ursuline Sisters listened to me with great interest, and the sisters who had left Cuba when their school was taken over by the

Castro government were only interested in what had become of their chapel. I was happy to be able to tell them that the school now was taking care of some 4,000 students and the chapel had been turned into a library.

The sisters were interested, perhaps, because they were confronted every day by the spectacle of the shanty-town at their door. In the shelter of the walls which surrounded the school grounds, makeshift shelters had been constructed so that it was in effect a village which was growing up around them. They had started a school for the children of the poor in the shadow of the academy which was taking care of the daughters of the well-to-do.

The desert village I visited with Father Hessler was quite another matter. We had driven for hours out of Mexico City, with the Catholic Relief Service nurse who was helping to distribute food which the CRS had received from United States surplus commodities. Personnel and freight charges were paid for by the CRS.

It was not really a village but a few houses surrounding a church in the middle of a desert which was cold by night and scorching hot in the day. The homes were thatched huts, and American students had come for a few months to help build up a better water supply and put up some concrete block houses.

The church was locked and the church yard was a waste land. Many small depressions dotted the church yard—the resting places of buried infants, their graves dug by their parents, their funerals unattended by a priest.

"Is Mass said here?" I wondered, and the Indians shook their heads. "There is no money here," they said. There was no teacher, no radio, though there had been, and when Father Hessler told them that I had just been to Fidel Castro's Cuba, they gathered around me, their eyes upon me, hungering and thirsting for some word, some news, of what was happening. I could speak too little Spanish to communicate with them, though I tried, so Father spoke to them, and told them all I had seen. I will never forget their grave, gaunt faces.

It is for people such as these that Father Camilo Torres died.

What kind of a life is it that these guerrillas lead? There is some indication of it in a recent issue of *Ramparts,* which carries part of the diary of the Argentine doctor, Che Guevara, who left his country to care for the Indians of Bolivia, who joined Castro in Cuba and was with him through the invasion which left only twelve of the eighty-five revolutionists alive when they took to the mountains of Oriente province and began their life of hiding, helped by the campesinos, helping them in turn and teaching them, and treating them with scrupulous honesty and respect.

"Our mission," Che Guevara wrote in his account of the initial encounters in Cuba where he lived among the peasants, "is to bring out the best in everyone and to turn everyone into a revolutionary." He tells of the first time he had to choose

27

between "my devotion to medicine and my duty as a revolutionary soldier." He had begun his revolutionary career while working among the Indians of Bolivia, while in exile from the Argentine, his own country. "There at my feet were a knapsack full of medicines and a box of ammunition. I could not possibly carry both of them. They were too heavy. I picked up the box of ammunition, leaving the medicine."

And the same, I am afraid, would happen to the priest dedicated to working with the guerrillas. He would turn to the ammunition.

It is impossible not to link the deaths of Che Guevara and Camilo Torres, because the story of both is influencing the thinking of students, workers, revolutionaries, and now missionary priests, bishops and clergy in the Third World.

Both were young and of heroic stature. One a doctor, the other a teacher of sociology in the University of Bogota. One kept diaries and reminiscences of his active days in the field of combat. The other wrote platforms, manifestos, documents, many of them contained in this book.

The problem remains—how to make the nonviolent means towards a new social order, "the new heavens and a new earth wherein justice flourishes," as stirring, as inspiring, as the lives of the heroes of *war,* whether civil war, guerrilla war, or international wars in which ordinary men are caught up.

Priests and missionaries by steady, patient work are trying to build up unions of workers, cooperatives, land settlements — building a new society within the shell of the old. But this is slow work, involving only a few hundred, and compromised by its association with the "oligarchy."

How to lift the concept of brotherhood ("all men are brothers") to the plane of the supernatural, so that we will get away from that childish and simplistic picture of friend and enemy, the black aspect and the white aspect of a situation, that division which is so fatal to brotherly love.

Human nature being what it is (and how often we hear that phrase), only the grace of God can help here. "In Your hand are power and might; Yours it is to give everything grandeur and strength." And "everything" in this situation means all those little acts, the daily work and suffering and forbearance and loving kindness which are necessary to build up the union, the little republic, the commune. And I am thinking of the Farm Workers' Union of Cesar Chavez, the *little republics* of Colombia, and the communes of China.

"We are trained to offer no resistance," one of the leaders of the United States Rural Workers said in an interview this week. "If we are attacked on the picket line, we do not answer with violence."

In the case of the republics of Colombia, the work of building up such enclaves is a non-violent work, but when they are attacked the peasants resist.

"When we choose the poor, we can always be sure of not going wrong," Father Henry de Lubac, S.J., wrote. "When we choose an ideology we can never be sure of not being at least partly wrong. When we have complied with an ideology, we can never be sure of having taken the right course. When we choose the poor, we are always sure, doubly sure of having made a good choice. We have chosen like Jesus. And we have chosen Jesus."

I must say that this introduction which I was asked to write is a hard assignment. I am a pacifist, I am on the side of the non-violent revolution. One is not pacifist if he is thinking only in terms of the present war which is going on in Vietnam. It is said that it is only human to take sides. And yet we are told in the Gospel to love our enemies. We are told that all men are brothers, and that "God wills that all men be saved" (though some will be saved as though by fire, St. Paul adds). We are told not to resist evil, and that if men take our coat, we are to give up our cloak also.

Somewhere Kierkegaard has written that Christianity is "the greatest wound ever inflicted on mankind." St. Bonaventure, recognizing the fantastic paradox which Christianity presents with its "royal road of the Cross," ("in the cross is joy of spirit") did not hesitate to beg for this wound. "Pierce, O most sweet Lord Jesus, my inmost soul with the most joyous and healthful wound of Thy love." A fatal wound.

Jesus says we must give up our lives to find them. To lay down our lives for our brothers, not take the sword against them. "All men are brothers."

Now two Maryknoll priests and a sister choose to leave their mission in Guatemala and at the present time are with the guerrillas who bear the name of "The Camilo Torres Front." We must pray they do not make the choice of Che who chose the box of ammunition rather than the medicines.

In 1876 Dostoevsky wrote a letter to a friend which contained the idea which was the basis of his "Legend of The Grand Inquisitor," that famous chapter in *The Brothers Karamazov:*

"In the temptation of the devil three colossal world ideas have become merged," writes Dostoevsky, "and here 18 centuries have passed, but there are no ideas more difficult, i.e., more trying, than these and even now no one can resolve them. 'The stones and bread' symbolize the present-day social question, and environment. This is not a prophecy, it always has been so. 'Rather than go to the ravaged poor, who from hunger and oppression look more like beasts than like men, rather than go and start preaching to the hungry abstention from sins, humility, chastity, is it not better first to feed them? That would be humane. Even before You, people came to preach, but why, You are the Son of God; the whole world has waited for You with impatience; then act as one who is superior to all in mind and justice, give them all food, make them secure, give them a social structure so that they might always have bread and order, and then ask them their sins. Then, if they sin, they will be un-

Dostoevsky, His Life and Work by Constantin Mochulsky, translated, with an introduction by Michael A. Minihan, Princeton Universtiy Press, 1967.

grateful, but now they commit sin from hunger. It is sinful even to ask them.

" 'You are the Son of God—therefore You can do everything. Here are stones—you see how many. You have only to command and the stones will be turned into bread. Command then that from now on the earth bring forth without toil, teach men such a science or teach them such an order, so that their life might henceforth be provided for. Can you really not believe that the greatest vices and miseries of man have resulted from hunger, cold, poverty and from the impossible struggle for existence.'

"Here is the first idea which the evil spirit proposed to Christ. You must agree that it is difficult to deal with it. Contemporary socialism in Europe, and with us too, everywhere puts Christ aside and concerns itself above all else with bread, calls upon science and declares that the cause of all man's miseries is poverty alone, struggle for existence, 'the environment has gone bad.'

"To this Christ answered: 'Not by bread alone does man live' . . .

The death of Father Camilo Torres leaves us torn with sorrow, for him, that his life was so short, and for the students who needed him so, and for us all who think of him as someone who truly wished to give his life for his brothers and who knew of no other way to do it save by joining his life to theirs, and making their cause his own.

But we must remember this. When was ever a non-violent solution offered as an alternative to violent revolution? Did Fidel Castro ever hear of non-violence in the schools he attended—schools taught by Jesuits or Christian Brothers? Did Camilo Torres ever hear of the teachings of Gandhi in the diocesan seminary in Bogota, Colombia, or at Louvain? Or did he know of Martin Luther King?

Christ is our Peace and He told Peter that those who took the sword would perish by the sword. He told us to love our enemies and He also said that our worst enemies would be those of our own household. Without these teachings of Jesus, what hope is there for the Church in Latin America?

Was it of this those sixteen bishops were thinking when they wrote their pastoral letter? Since the teachings of Jesus were never taught to the guerrillas, never taught to the poor, nor to the rich, to the students in the colleges nor the seminarians—those teachings which told us all to love our enemies, to do good to those who despitefully use us, to give up our cloak also when we have been robbed of our coat, well then, let us give up hope of achieving brotherhood by the new way, and bow the head to what comes. But never let us take sides in the sense that we are on the side of the rich, of the successful, the respectable, those who have money and can support the schools, the missionary effort. Rather lose all, as the church has so often lost all in the past, recognizing that persecution is deserved and undeserved too. Is the servant above his Master?

And yet what a paradox is presented to us by Christ's message. We are not to turn stones into

bread, we are not to pay attention to our lives—
what we will eat and what we will wear—yet Christ
had compassion on the multitude and multiplied
the loaves and fishes. That He did not do it more
than twice meant that we were to work those problems out ourselves. He knew we needed bread for
our comfort as well as for our growth. He raised a
little girl to life and told those around to "give
her to eat." St. Peter's wife, cured of fever, rose
and served Christ and the disciples. He fed them
the paschal lamb, the salad and the bread at the
last supper and later gave them Himself in bread
and wine. After He rose from the dead He fed
them by the shore, where Peter in his grief had
gone back to his nets. He fed them honey ("taste
and see that the Lord is sweet") and the fresh fish
which He fried for them. Jesus Christ knew that
we needed bread before we could know ourselves
as men. Indeed we knew Him in the breaking of
bread. And it was over this same bread that divi-
sions first came, disputes and dissensions. Those
who spoke Greek complained that their widows,
their poor were being overlooked in the daily distribution of food and that those who spoke the
language of the Jews were favored. Already there
had been death in their midst, the death of Sap-
phira and Ananias who went in for trickery in pre-
tending to give their money to the poor. (One
wonders what really happened to give rise to this
tale.)

Yes, Jesus Christ knew we needed bread. What
we need today is faith that He can multiply what

we are able to get by our own puny efforts, so that we do not have to rely on force to take over "the means of production."

Martin Luther King also knew that men need bread and he died for his faith that only non-violent means will obtain it. He had gone to Memphis, Tennessee, where the Garbage Collectors' Union was on strike for the living wage which would enable them to pay for their daily bread, to join in procession with them, to call attention to their plight. It was a march to voice their demands, but it was also a supplicatory procession. How could brother close his heart against his brother in need?

Over and over again Martin Luther King had risked his life in opposing war, the war which was going on in Vietnam, and the war between races, the war between classes at home. He, too, like Camilo Torres, had come from the privileged professional class, had studied at Boston University and Harvard, had never suffered hunger as his black brothers had for so long. The very honors that were heaped upon him, the Nobel prize, the publication of all his writings; the beauty of his private life, with his lovely wife and his children, made the whites hate him and fight him the more. His life indeed was a long continuing martyrdom. He was spat upon, beaten, jailed. His home was bombed. And finally, on Thursday in Passion week, the night before the day celebrated as the day of the seven sorrows of the Virgin Mother of God, he was shot through the throat and his eloquent voice was stilled.

Martin Luther King, we ask your prayers that we learn more to overcome ourselves, and to learn the violence we need to impose upon ourselves in overcoming righteous wrath against the oppressor, and so grow in non-violence. Father Camilo Torres, pray for us, that we may have your courage in offering our lives for our brothers. And may God's light shine upon you both, and may you rest in peace.

April, 1968

the
colombia
of
camilo torres

by virginia m. o'grady

Colombia is unique in Latin America as the best
example of a two-party system. Early in the nineteenth century the various political currents in the
country were fused into the two main streams of
Liberalism and Conservatism. These streams were
consolidated into parties between 1821 and 1848.
Their points of view were hostile and the leaders
were bitter in their mutual opposition. In time the
parties became the principal instigators and chan-
nels of violence. But political participation was the
privilege of the upper class, unknown to the illiterate masses.

Like the rest of the underdeveloped world, Colombia is living through a period of acute unrest.
Its instability is increased by the continued existence of a highly stratified conservative society
headed by a powerful oligarchic class. For well
over a century the oligarchy has monopolized the
country's politics and wealth. Wealth has enabled

it to control the nation's economic policies and to move with ease in the circles of international power. Politics has been its favorite pastime, a game that has caused unspeakable tragedies to the Colombian people. By 1957 the political situation had degenerated to such degree that Colombians were faced with the imperative choice of compromise or national suicide. The catalyst was a military dictator.

Throughout the last century and well into the twentieth Colombia experienced a period of *caciquismo,* of crude alliances between landowners, the clergy, and the military, of economic feudalism, religious fanaticism, and party intransigency. But the most prominent feature in its political history was violence. Independence was won in 1810. From that year until 1903 Colombia suffered ten revolutions and seventy uprisings. The bloody upheavals and narrow partisan hatreds became regular features of Colombian national life. In general the civil wars were fought over principles rather than personalities because, from the very beginning, Colombians were determined to maintain civilian government.

At the dawn of the twentieth century Colombia was the victim of a holocaust which lasted a thousand days. Then the fighting stopped. For the next forty-five years Liberals and Conservatives were able to co-exist, and the moderates of both parties came to a realization that they had no irreconcilable differences.

After World War I Colombia felt the birth-pangs

of modernization. Rural and urban labor grew dissatisfied with the status quo. A new phase of violence began and was aggravated by the Great Depression. Wages plummeted, prices soared, and strikes were brutally suppressed. But the masses were at least beginning to make themselves heard. The country was ripe for revolution. Sensing the danger, the political oligarchies joined hands to halt the "catastrophic" change.

[Colombia's political history marked a decisive turn in 1930: the triumph of the Liberals meant an end to the forty-year rule of the Conservatives. The latter avenged their loss by advocating violence and death as preferable to hunger and subjection to Liberal rule. At this time the country's economy was seriously threatened because of a fall in foreign trade. Social unrest mounted. The national departments progressively fell prey to the madness of fierce vendettas, for in Colombia one is born either a Liberal or a Conservative. A slur on one's party is, in fact, a slur on one's family and on one's very name.

In forty years the Conservatives had managed to obtain a strong foothold in the countryside. Conservative landowners and the Church utterly dominated the lives of the peasants. It is no wonder, then, that the Liberal takeover resulted in a resurgence of partisan violence. But the oligarchs were not the victims. The dead and mutilated were ignorant peons who were instigated to murder and plunder by arrogant, uncompromising masters.]

[The Liberals, who were in the majority in 1930,

have remained a majority ever since—primarily because of the social and economic changes which have taken place in Colombia since the end of World War I. The party attracted to its ranks a heterogeneous group of people which included dissatisfied intellectuals, rising industrialists, and the opponents of the dominant and privileged position of the Church. But the very diversity of the party's composition threatened its unity. In the years after 1930 internecine struggles repeatedly thwarted the efforts of the Liberals. During this time Conservatives boycotted elections and fanned the flames of division within Liberal ranks.

After 1945 the Colombian political arena was dominated by two political giants. One, the leader of the left wing of the Liberal party, was Jorge Eliecer Gaitan. The other, Laureano Gomez y Castro, was an aristocrat of wealth and culture who incarnated privilege and the past. Gaitan, a charismatic figure and powerful agitator, was a non-conformist. He championed the cause of the oppressed and denounced the privileges of the oligarchy. His rise to fame was meteoric and his popularity extraordinary. He was a man of the masses and the symbol of Colombia's revolution. Gomez was the leader of the Conservatives and the terror of the *politicos.* He was an engineer who had become a newspaper publisher to further his political ambitions. He was the mastermind behind the maneuvers to harass the Liberal administration. His attacks were constant and ruthless.

In 1946 Colombia was torn by agitation, strikes,

and disorder. The Liberal government fell in mid 1945 and was replaced by a coalition government to avert civil war. The new government, known as the National Union, was headed by the internationally know Alberto Lleras Camargo.

The presidential elections of 1946 ended in victory for the Conservatives. It was a case of a divided majority losing the day to a united minority. Although they were in power, the Conservatives were tormented by insecurity and renewed their campaign of violence. Murder and savagery reigned in Colombia while a horrified world looked on. In the meantime, Gaitan gained steadily in popularity. It was Gaitan, in fact, who posed the greatest threat to the future of Conservatism in Colombia. His relentless attacks on the coalition government caused its disintegration in March of 1948.

Colombia was racked by social and economic problems. Inflation, black marketeering, and a rise in the cost of living drove the masses to despair. Violence erupted throughout the country. The final explosion came on April 9, 1948 when Jorge Eliecer Gaitan was assassinated. This was the infamous *bogotazo*, when the people demanded 'a social revolution in brutal terms.'

On that monstrous 'Black Friday' the 'Athens of the New World' was destroyed. Colombians had made an agonized call for change to an insensitive oligarchy. Twelve hundred lost their lives in a week of rioting. But the coalition government was restored, and the violence continued. Fierce Conservatives went on a rampage and Liberals were not slow to retaliate. The government used the police and army to harass the opposition. Armed guerrillas in the hills attacked the government forces and undefended villages.

Because of Liberal abstention from the polls, the Conservatives won the elections of 1949. Laureano Gomez became President and established a dictatorship. He was an admirer of Franco's Spain, an ardent advocate of *hispanidad* and *falangismo*. He favored business and industry while tightening the control on labor. The coffee industry boomed and the oligarchy grew richer in a time of plenty. But the masses dwelt in misery and privation. Violence continued unabated; the government seemed powerless to suppress it. The Liberals were practically destroyed by internal struggles, and the Conservatives were "split over the spoils of victory." Colombia needed a savior.

In a bloodless coup on June 13, 1953, Lieutenant General Gustavo Rojas Pinilla took over the government. He had the support of the majority of Colombians. During his first few months in power there was a decline in violence and a gradual return to normalcy. But in a short time his regime became a dictatorship. It was an interlude in the political development of Colombia. It came into being because the traditional parties failed to adapt to the revolutionary changes of the times and refused to heed the demands of the masses.

By 1957 nationwide dissatisfaction with Rojas Pinilla was complete. He had collided with the Church and faced the solid opposition of the Liberals and Conservatives. When he attempted to extend his presidential term to 1962 he was forced to resign and go into exile. The violence which he had succeeded in curtailing during the first months of his administration broke out again in the countryside. Shortly before its renewed outbreak, however, the Liberals took the initiative in negotiations for a bipartisan government. Liberals and Conservatives would share power, policy-making, and responsibility. Rojas Pinilla's despotic rule and ineptitude forced the traditional parties to come to an agreement. His dictatorship was a subversion of institutional order. While Colombians lost their lives in senseless fighting, Rojas Pinilla's best efforts only hastened the ruin of the nation's traditions and economy.

The rapprochement between Liberals and Conservatives was ultimately agreed to by Alberto Lleras Camargo and Laureano Gomez. It is interesting to note that public opinion was far ahead of the national leaders in realizing the advantage of compromise. Efforts were made by the people to stimulate understanding at the grass-roots level. Throughout 1955 and 1956 the Liberal and Conservative leaders negotiated the terms of the bipartisan experiment which was to be known as the National Front. The pact between the two parties became a reality in July, 1957. Its two most important principles were a sharing of command at all levels of government, and alternation in office between the Liberals and Conservatives. Alberto Lleras Camargo was hailed as the author of the experiment. It was designed to put an end to violence and corruption. Since 1948, 300,000 Colombians had lost their lives. The economy was suffering from a corruption of public morals and the wanton destruction of vast tracts of land and even of entire communities.

On December 1, 1957, Colombians went to the polls for the first popular elections since 1949. It was the biggest turn-out in the history of the nation. The National Front was approved and Colombia entered a period of 'democratic convalescence.' Four months later, the Liberal Alberto Lleras Camargo won the presidential elections. He was fully aware of the enormity of his task. In his own words, he would have to be 'a magician, prophet, redeemer, savior and pacifier who can transform a ruined republic into a prosperous one.' It was unfortunate that the professional politicians could not rise to the occasion: intra-party factionalism plagued the Lleras administration. Nevertheless, military expenditures were curtailed, and appropriations for agriculture, education, health, and public works were nearly doubled. But a new wave of violence swept over the countryside. Defenseless peasants were massacred by armed bandits dressed as army regulars. The government blamed the traditional parties for instigating the killings. A few years of coalition government could not eradicate the decades of violence which had dominated the Colombian political scene. What was new was that vicious competition was severe now within the parties rather than between them, which caused endless confusion. The split within the Conservative ranks was along personal lines, while that of the Liberals was along ideological lines. Among the most important factions of the Liberal party was the Liberal Revolutionary Movement (*Movimiento Revolucionario Liberal*—MRL), which was very critical of the administration and vehemently opposed to the principle of alternation. Of all the existing factions, the MRL stood out for its commitment to revolution.

The presidential elections of 1962 were won by the Conservative Guillermo Leon Valencia. Colombia's unusual experiment in "controlled democracy" was safeguarded for another four years, but an evaluation of its first years of life would be anything but optimistic. Between 1958 and 1962 Lleras Camargo lived in constant tension trying to keep the country at peace and the National Front from collapsing. The bipartisan government was an artificial arrangement fashioned primarily to put an end to violence. In this, its main objective, it was a failure. Lleras' successor was faced with much the same difficulties.

At the heart of Colombia's problems is the fact that politics and the economy are the monopoly of the oligarchy, of twenty-four powerful families who refuse to accept the need for profound structural change. There were those who believed that bipartisan government would bring a revolution from the top. But the political elites have preferred to exhaust themselves in party feuding, and seem to be totally insensitive to the needs of the masses. Per-

45

haps the most unfortunate aspect of the National Front is that it increased factionalism within the parties. The days go by, the country's needs increase, and the parties continue their intrigues. Colombia's problems are acute, and her people are suffering. The country is on the threshold of a revolution.

The rise of Camilo Torres must be seen against this background. This was the Colombia which saw his birth on February 3, 1929. His parents, Camilo Torres Umana and Isabel Restrepo de Torres, were members of the oligarchic class. Their son attended the Liceo Recaurte and received a Bachelor's degree from the Liceo Cervantes. His vocation to the priesthood led him to complete his studies at the Archdiocesan Seminary of Bogota.

Camilo Torres obtained a Masters' degree in Social Science from the University of Louvain, Belguim. At Louvain he studied under Jacques Leclercq, Charles Moeller, Jean Ladriere, and Francois Houtart. He was appointed Vice Rector of the Latin American College, a seminary founded by the Belgian bishops to train priests for Latin America.

On his return to Colombia, Torres was appointed chaplain to the National University. He was profoundly moved by the plight of his fellow-countrymen, and shared his views with the students of the University. He combined his religious duties with participation in student strikes and progressive political movements. Because of acute ideological differences with the Church hierarchy, Torres was removed from the chaplaincy in February, 1961. He had lasted in the post less than two years. The University then appointed him professor in the Faculty of Sociology and the School of Economic Sciences. He taught courses at the University until September, 1962. His relations with the hierarchy and with his religious superiors grew increasingly strained. Torres took a position in the School of Public Administration where he remained until May, 1965. At this time, he decided to abandon the priesthood and his position as Dean of the Institute of Social Administration. To his friends and political colleagues he announced his intention to direct a guerrilla movement.

Camilo Torres' revolutionary career was a brief one. In the year preceding his death he organized a new political movement—the United Front—made up in the main of intellectuals and students in urban centers. But he realized the futility of armed uprisings in the cities and saw a reservoir of power in the disenfranchised peasantry. It was this which prompted him to join the *guerrilleros* in the mountains, the armed enclaves of resistance to the government which exist throughout Colombia.

Torres declared himself a revolutionary because he was a Catholic and because he was a priest. He felt that to live the life of a Christian with integrity every man must be concerned with the concrete needs of his neighbor. Moreover, in the case of Colombia, Torres saw the necessity for radical change in the basic social and economic structures. On these issues he collided with the Church hierarchy. The conservative Cardinal Concha Cordoba condemned Torres' platform for social reform as 'pernicious and erroneous.' It was at this point, in July of 1965, that Torres requested and received release from his priestly duties.

Camilo Torres was cognizant of the need to integrate all groups interested in revolutionary change into a United Popular Front so that the take-over of power would be more effective. But the United Front failed because of the apathy of the masses, the harassment of the government, and the lack of cohesion of the revolutionary forces. Moreover, the Front was dominated increasingly by Communists, which caused the withdrawal of the Christian Democratic Party and the Christian Labor movement (CLASC) in September, 1965.

Torres grew exasperated with the traditional parties and the behavior of their leaders and became convinced that only armed rebellion could offer a way out. His next step was to join the Army of National Liberation (ELN). The ELN continues the violence which over the last twenty years has claimed innumerable lives. It is bent on destroying the traditional ruling class. Fighting with the ELN, Camilo Torres met death in the town of El Carmen on Tuesday, February 15, 1966, just two months after joining the guerrillas. In the mountains of Colombia government bullets ended the life of the thirty-seven-year old priest turned *guerrillero*.

At the time of his death Torres was a nationally prominent figure, a rebel priest preaching a popular social revolution. His principal targets were the oligarchy, the leaders of the traditional parties, the economic elites, and a good part of the Church. Torres represented a new voice within the Colombian Church: that of the younger clergymen and dedicated laymen concerned with implementing the social doctrine of the Church. They are opposed by the conservative hierarchy. They see the urgent need for "radical renovation of the power relationships within Colombian society." Structural reforms are crucial; paternalism must be replaced with participation by all Colombians in decision-making. Change will not come easily to Colombia because of the prevailing sense of distrust which exists in the society and because of the "rootlessness, hopelessness, bitterness, and violence among the *lumpenproletariat* of the cities and the forgotten peasantry in the countryside."

To attempt to judge Camilo Torres would be misleading and presumptuous. Rather, he must be regarded as Canon Houtart suggests: "Even if we cannot approve of it, Camilo's gesture has a prophetic meaning: to recall to his people their sin. Let us hope that at least some of them will understand."

his platform
and his
messages

The remainder of this book is a collection of the writing of Camilo Torres made by John Alvarez Garcia and Christian Restrepo Calle. It was originally published by Ediciones Carpel, Antorcha, Medellin, Colombia. Two short statements by the editors and a description of the United Front precede Torres' political platform and his messages to the Colombian people.

preface

I would follow the directives of the Pontiffs of the Church any day rather than those of the pontiffs of our ruling class. (CAMILO TORRES)

The main purpose of this book is to keep alive the memory of Camilo Torres, a revolutionary hero who gave his life for an ideal that continues to be misunderstood even by some of his closest followers.

His ideals, which are the ideals of all free men in Colombia, must not be forgotten. His work, which has scarcely begun, must be the starting point for the new generations which will see it through to its completion.

Social protest, discontent, and the thirst for justice were embodied in Camilo Torres. He was a light in the darkness which enveloped the Colombian people.

J.A.C.

51

introduction

Camilo Torres Restrepo was entirely a priest. He shunned the special favors and distinctions which are the compensation of those who obediently submit to systems promising advancement. He knew how to fill his life and behavior with love, to such a degree that not even death seemed too high a price to pay to justify his choice.

He was so moved by the lot of the "marginals," of the indigent, and of the poor, that he committed himself to finding a way for their liberation. Thus, armed with truth, with knowledge of the national realities, with youth, and with his priesthood, he plunged into the fight.

In 1963 he held a meeting at his home, which was located at the north of Bogota, with leaders of the M.R.L., of the Democratic Christian Socialist Party, of the New Press group, and of independents. The purpose of the meeting was to look for a common road which, putting aside all pettiness and particular points of view, would serve to join in action all the groups opposing the existing system.

The meeting eventually bore favorable results. In February, 1965, Torres composed a platform for popular unity. He gave a copy to the political leader of Tolima, Jaime Corredor Arjona, who in turn gave it to a labor leader of Medellin who at the time was in Ibague. The original copy of the manuscript remained in Medellin, where it became the basis for discussion among a group of youthful political leaders who, at Camilo Torres' suggestion, carefully analyzed the original platform and made some additions and corrections.

In mid March, 1965, Torres was invited to Medellin by the youth of Antioquia. After a number of talks, a dinner was held in his honor at the "Fonda Antioquena" of the Parque de Bolivar. Delegates of the youth of the M.R.L., of the Christian Democrats, of the independents, of the two wings of Communism, of the Liberals, and of the Conservatives were all present. Camilo Torres read a corrected version of his original platform. It was accepted and made public that very same night of March 17, and given to all the youth and distributed among the poor of Colombia.

Camilo Torres' *via crucis* began that same night. He was accused by the oligarchy of Medellin and forced to flee from the ESAP *(Escuela Superior de Administracion Publica)*. He was the victim of calumny and misinterpretations; he was repudiated by the ecclesiastical hierarchy. Camilo Torres was forced to take refuge on a hill—the same hill on which he met his death on February 15, 1966.

But Camilo Torres has not really died, because he is an idea and ideas never die. The text of his original platform, as corrected by Torres himself and signed by those attending the dinner at the "Fonda Antioquena," is reprinted in this book, along with all his messages to the Colombian people.

C.R.C.

THE UNITED FRONT

The United Front of the People was born as an answer to the exploitation of man by man, to identify itself with the masses and give them an awareness of their power, to direct the people toward revolution.

The United Front of the People is the result of several years of experience and reflection; it was not just an invention of Father Camilo. Other countries which have obtained their freedom have had as their moving force the organization of the exploited in a United Front. In Colombia Camilo was its promoter and its director, not its *caudillo*. He never presumed to be that. Camilo acted with detachment, in a rational and scientific manner.

As a revolutionary, Camilo could count on the strongest force: the force of reason which is the force of the people. Never in the history of the world have the people made a mistake, and Camilo died for the people (if this really means dying).

One obvious fact about the United Front is that

it is the mass movement which was created in the shortest time. In less than two months the United Front of the People came into being. And its ideological foundations were being propounded by a group of university professors, intellectuals, and students. The United Front was born in the universities. From the classrooms it radiated out to the entire country.

The United Front of the People hopes to be the instrument which will unite the masses. It desires an immediate alliance with the opposition, elimininating the discrepancies and working on the points that are held in common.

Through Camilo, the United Front of the People presented a Platform of Action which synthesizes its objectives.

The United Front is not only an alliance of parties. It is the organization of the whole people. It is not the property of an individual but of the Colombian people. They must be able to resolve the difficulties which will constantly appear. It struggles for the cohesion of the great masses; it aspires to be a center of radiation and not of division, to integrate the popular class with the national classes. It wishes to transform Colombia into a sociospiritual entity of dignity, individuality, and independence where the people will be, simultaneously, actors and spectators.

What is important is that the Colombian popular class continue always to advance without any steps backward, in spite of defections, false rumors, and treason. The decision of the poor, who do not want their children to accuse them in the future of having betrayed their historic and revolutionary vocation, is what will define the situation. Even though it will be a long struggle, what is important is that everyone who decides to take part in it will see it through to the end.

Religious News Service Photo

camilo torres

the platform of camilo torres

march 17, 1965

To all Colombians, to the popular class, to the middle class, to the organizations for communal action, to the unions, cooperatives, societies for mutual aid, peasant leagues, labor organizations and Indians, to all the discontented, to men and women, to youth, to all those not aligned with the traditional political parties, and to the new parties, we present the following platform in order to give unity to the Colombian popular class, based on concrete objectives.

MOTIVES

1) At present the decisions that are necessary for Colombian politics to be oriented in favor of the majority and not of the minority must be made by those in power.

2) Those who currently hold power belong to a minority which also controls the economy and which is responsible for the fundamental decisions made in national politics.

59

3) This minority will never make decisions which will adversely affect its own interests.

4) The decisions which are imperative for the socio-economic and political development of the country and of the majority of the people will necessarily affect the interests of the economic minority.

5) These circumstances make it absolutely necessary to change the structure of the political power, so that the organized majorities will be heard in decision-making.

6) There does not exist in Colombia today a social power capable of laying the foundations for a new political power which is so urgently needed.

7) At present the majorities reject the traditional political parties and the existing system, but they do not have an adequate political apparatus of their own ready to take power.

8) The political apparatus which must be organized must be pluralist in nature, reaping maximum advantage from the support of the new parties, of the dissatisfied sectors of the traditional parties, of the non-political organizations, and of the masses in general. It must be based on technical planning and principles of action, rather than built around a leader, if cliques, demagoguery, and personalism are to be avoided.

OBJECTIVES

I. AGRARIAN REFORM

Land will be owned by those who work on it directly. The government will appoint agrarian inspectors who will hand over titles to the peasant laborers who fulfill these requisites. The government will be able to require that the land be exploited by communal and cooperative systems, in keeping with a national agrarian plan, and providing, as well, credit facilities and technical assistance.

Land will be bought from no one. All land which is deemed necessary for the common good will be expropriated without indemnization. Subsistence agriculture will disappear gradually and be replaced by commercial agriculture.

II. URBAN REFORM

1) Urban reform will be in keeping with the methods and effects of the agrarian reform, and will be coordinated with all the plans of the Institute of Land Credit, the Central Mortgage Bank, Societies of Architects, Colombian Chamber of Construction, etc., as well as with all the entities and firms in charge of public services.

2) All home-dwellers in towns and cities will be owners of the houses they inhabit. Persons who rent a house as a means to support themselves will be able to continue to do so, even though they do not live in it, if they are able to prove that this is their situation.

3) The owner of any room, which, in the judgment of the urban reform office, is not being sufficiently used, will be fined. Income derived from such fines will be invested by the State in its housing program.

4) Empty lots in urban and suburban areas will

be expropriated and utilized by the housing program.

III. The Reform of Business

Free enterprise will be abolished and replaced by cooperative and communitarian enterprise. As a first step, all voting in the general meetings of incorporated companies will be done in terms of the persons who are associated with the company and not of the capital represented by the shares. All the workers will be able to be shareholders. They will be organized in unions and as such will be able to participate in the direction and administration of the companies. This participation of labor on an equal footing with capital in all opportunities that present themselves could be direct or indirect, depending on the judgment of the unions themselves.

Pluralism in union organization will be encouraged, always allowing for the free choice of the workers. Freedom for the organization of labor will be respected in keeping with international labor organization agreements.

IV. Cooperatives

The creation of cooperatives for credit and savings, marketing, production, construction, consumption, etc. will be greatly encouraged. Cooperatives will be institutionalized by the State and will operate freely in keeping with the democratic planning established by the popular organizations.

V. Communal Action

As part of the process of democratic planning, communal action will be fostered in both rural and urban sectors. Municipal life will be revivified. The councilmen will be freely elected by the members of the community. In a word, the municipalities will become living cells of the nation.

VI. PLANNING

A compulsory, overall plan will be established aimed at substituting imports and diversifying and increasing exports. In the shortest possible time it is hoped that only those capital goods will be imported which will contribute unquestionably to national development.

In any case, the policy of foreign commerce will be directly related to the growth and development of Latin America's integration.

VII. TAX POLICY

A progressive tax will be levied on all persons earning between one thousand and five thousand *pesos* monthly. All income in excess of five thousand *pesos* (in 1965) which is not invested in areas sanctioned by the official plan will have to be turned over in its entirety to the State. No institution will be exempt from paying taxes.

Salaries amounting up to five thousand *pesos* monthly (in 1965) will not be taxed if they are family salaries. If they are not, they will be subject to the existing regulations.

VIII. MONETARY POLICY

No new money will be issued unless the objective is to enhance those sectors of production which will make possible short or long-term transactions. The

Colombian State approves the gold standard for international transactions.

IX. Nationalizations

1) Banks, hospitals, clinics, laboratories, pharmacies, and the exploitation of natural resources will belong to the State.

2) Public transportation will be operated by co-operative and communitarian firms. If this is not possible the State will take over.

3) The press, radio, TV, and the movies will be free but subject to the control of the State with an eye to the common good.

4) The State will make possible free education for all Colombians, respecting the ideology of the parents until the end of secondary education, and that of the student himself after secondary school. Education will be compulsory until the completion of secondary or technical education. Penal sanctions will be imposed on parents who fail to comply with the obligation to educate their children. The financing of education will be provided for in the official investment plan by the increase in taxation.

5) Oil will be exploited by the Colombian State so long as it is able to finance the industry. Concessions to foreign oil companies will not be made unless the following conditions exist:

    a) That refineries are established simultaneously in Colombia.

    b) That 80% of the industry remain in the hands of the State.

    c) That the entire oil industry be handed over

to the State within a period not exceeding ten years.

d) That the salaries of Colombian employees and workers be at least equal to those of foreigners in the same job categories.

X. International Relations

Colombia will have diplomatic and commercial relations with all the countries of the world.

X. Public Health

All persons in professions connected with health will be employees of the State.

A first step will be to assign to each professional a number of families in keeping with the size of the Colombian population and the number of professionals.

The State will give social assistance to all Colombians.

XII. Family Policy

Parents who abandon their children will be subject to legal punishment. The law will protect wives and children and provide effective sanctions.

XIII. Social Crimes

Besides the crimes already covered by our legislation and those mentioned in connection with the abandonment of the home, the following will also be regarded as social crimes: usury, monopoly, speculation, the flight of capital, contraband, defamation by the press, radio, TV, or the movies, misleading public opinion by false news or incomplete or tendentious information.

XIV. The Armed Forces

The budget for instruments of violence will be reduced to the minimum. All Colombians, both men and women, will have to render a two-year period of civic service after their eighteenth birthday. Military service, therefore, will be replaced by this civic service.

XV. University Reform

The University will be autonomous and will be organized as a community of professors, students, and alumni whose aim is the propagation of culture. The University must not be victimized by partisan politics, by the Army, or by the clergy. Its specific task, within the realm of universal culture, will be to study and to attempt to resolve national problems, in keeping with the peculiar characteristics of the country.

XVI. Legislation Regarding the
    Indigenous Population

The existing legislation regarding the indigenous population will be abolished. The Indian will be completely integrated into national life. He will have the same civic, cultural, and political rights and duties as the rest of the citizens.

IMMEDIATE ACTION

The final objective is the creation of a pluralist political apparatus, not of a new party, which will be capable of assuming power.

1) It is necessary to organize a movement from the bottom to the top which will guarantee individual and group adherence to this platform.

2) This platform will be distributed and explained to obtain individual and social adherence to

it during the months of March, April, and May, 1965, by the militants of movements that are in agreement with it.

3) All those who support this platform will be grouped in a *United Front of Popular Movements* which will reflect their unity of action as regards the ideology and specific programs of each group and party.

4) Committees for action will be formed in each municipality or neighborhood grouping all those who adhere to the platform. A leader and his substitute for each committee will be elected.

5) On May 31, 1965, departmental and district meetings will be held bringing together the leaders of the local committees in the capital of each department or district. At these meetings delegates will be elected for a meeting in Bogota.

6) The delegates elected at the departmental and district meetings will assemble in Bogota on July 20, 1965 to plan the immediate objectives of the United Front and its position vis-a-vis the presidential elections.

7) At this meeting a political committee will also be elected on which all interested movements and the natural regions of the country will be represented. Its purpose will be to coordinate the campaigns of the United Front.

8) Any project that is launched must count on the initiative and effort of the people organized for communal action in peasant leagues, labor unions. student and professional organizations, political parties, etc.

messages

REASONS WHY I WILL NOT
PARTICIPATE IN THE ELECTIONS

The Platform of the United Front of the Colombian People as a revolutionary tactic takes no position in regard to the electoral struggle.

In order to make possible the union of the revolutionaries, we must emphasize all those things which unite us and try to overlook the things that separate us. If the question of the elections presents a barrier to our union, it is better not to ask it, especially since we have no certainty that the elections will be held at all.

If I were in favor of the elections, the logical thing would be for us to prepare a slate and for me, personally, to become a candidate.

I believe this would mean the creation of a new political group which would divide the opposition even further. Such a result would run contrary to my main hope of uniting the Colombian popular class.

I do not consider myself a representative of the Colombian popular class, nor leader of the United Front, nor leader of the Colombian revolution, because I have not been elected by the people. I do hope to be accepted by the people as a *servant of the revolution.*

As long as the United Front does not elect its leaders I am not its chief, except in specific cases where members of the Front decide to the contrary. As I do not intend to participate in the elections, I must explain to the people what led me to this decision. I have already mentioned that I do not want to divide the opposition even further. But there are other reasons for my action.

1) The existing voting system forces the Colombian popular class to be divided into Liberals and Conservatives. And everything which divides a people is necessarily against its interests.

2) The electoral apparatus is in the hands of the oligarchy. Therefore, those who count the votes are the electors, the ones who determine the victor. The elections are decided more in the offices of the oligarchic government than in the voting booths.

3) As it is impossible to defeat those who control the electoral machinery and the positions of power, the opposition groups which enter Parliament could never effect the revolutionary changes that are so necessary. On the contrary, their presence in Parliament makes it easier for the oligarchy to say that democracy exists in Colombia because there is opposition.

4) It does not seem to me to be good revolu-

tionary education to tell the people with words that the oligarchy must be mistrusted, and with actions that they must turn over to the system one of man's most precious rights: his political opinion.

5) I believe that the time and money that are spent making up lists, discussing party lines, and deciding on political leaders, could better be employed by organizing and unifying the popular class at the base.

6) Should it so happen that the oligarchy make a mistake in counting the votes and that the opposition became the majority (as, for example, in the case of a new plebiscite), we know that, as was the case in the Argentine with the triumph of Peronism, the oligarchy could annul the elections and stage a coup d'etat. I do not think it would be difficult for an oligarchy which has not flinched in killing revolutionary leaders, in opening the country to violence, and in backing up military governments, to keep the opposition, should it become the majority as the result of elections, from gaining power. What is more, it has already been shown how it would be impossible for the opposition to become the majority.

Personally, I favor electoral abstention, but not passive abstention. What is needed is active, belligerent, and revolutionary abstention. Active abstention will mean the rejection of the whole system, including elections. This is why it must be politically motivated. The abstention will be belligerent because the revolutionary commandos will receive precise orders as to how they should act in

the electoral process. The abstention will be revolutionary because it will be used to organize and
unify the popular class for the final take-over of
power.   *P. Camilo Torres R.*

August 26, 1965

A MESSAGE TO CHRISTIANS

The political, religious, and social upheavals
which have occurred in recent times have undoubtedly caused much confusion in the minds of Colombia's Christians. In this decisive moment of our
history it is necessary, therefore, that we remain
steadfast in the essentials of our religion.

The most important Catholic precept is to love
one's neighbor. 'He who loves his neighbor obeys
the law,' (St. Paul, Romans, XIII, 8). For this love
to be true it must seek to be efficacious. If benefi-
cence, alms, a few free schools, a few nursing programs, in a word, what has been called "charity,"
does not suffice to feed the majority of the hungry,
to clothe the majority of the naked, to teach the
majority of the ignorant, then we must look for
more effective means of insuring the welfare of the
majority.

These means will not be sought by the privileged
minority which holds power because in general
such means oblige the minority to sacrifice its privileges. For example, if Colombia is to have more job
opportunities, it would be better to have the dollars
which are now sent abroad invested in the country.
With such investment new jobs would be created.
But as the Colombian *peso* suffers devaluation

72

every day, those who have money and power will never allow a prohibition on the exportation of money. By exporting it they are saved from the negative effects of devaluation.

It is necessary, therefore, to take power away from the privileged minority and give it to the poor majority. This, if it is done quickly, is the heart of a revolution. The Revolution can be peaceful if the minority does not resist with violence. The Revolution is, therefore, the way to get a government which will feed the hungry, clothe the naked, teach the ignorant, comply with the works of charity, and make possible a true love for our neighbors. This is why the Revolution is not only permitted but is obligatory for all Christians who see in it the most effective way of making possible a greater *love for all men*. It is true that 'there is no authority except that which comes from God' (St. Paul, Romans, XIII, 1). But St. Thomas says that, in the practical order, authority is given by the people.

When there is an authority which is against the people, that authority is not legitimate and it is called a tyranny. As Christians we can and we must fight against tyranny. Our present government is tyrannical because it is supported by only 20% of the electorate, and because decisions are made by the privileged minority.

The temporal defects of the Church must not scandalize us. The Church is human. What is important is to believe that it is also divine, and that if as Christians we comply with our obligation to love our neighbor by so doing we are reinforcing the Church.

I have put aside the privileges and duties of the clergy, but I have not stopped being a priest. I think I have given myself to the Revolution out of love for my neighbor. I have stopped offering Mass to live out the love for my neighbor in the temporal, economic, and social orders. When my neighbor no longer has anything against me, and when the revolution has been completed, then I will offer Mass again, if God so wills it. I believe that in this way I am following Christ's injunction. 'If you bring your offering to the altar and there remember that your brother has something against you, leave your offering on the altar and go and be reconciled first with your brother, and then return and offer your gift' (St. Matthew, V, 23-24).

After the Revolution we Christians will have the peace of mind which will come from knowing that we established a system which is grounded in the love of neighbor.

The struggle will be long. Let us begin today . . .

Camilo Torres

August 3, 1965

MESSAGE TO THE COMMUNISTS

Because of the traditional relations between Christians and Marxists, and between the Church and the Communist Party, it is quite likely that erroneous suspicions and suppositions will arise regarding the relations of Christians and Marxists within the United Front, and of a priest and the Communist Party.

74

This is why I want to clarify to the Colombian people my relations with the Communist Party and its position within the United Front.

I have said that I am a revolutionary as a Colombian, as a sociologist, as a Christian, and as a priest. I believe that there are elements within the Communist Party which are genuinely revolutionary. Consequently, I cannot be anti-Communist either as a Colombian, as a sociologist, as a Christian, or as a priest.

I am not anti-Communist as a Colombian because anti-Communism in my country is bent on persecuting the dissatisfied, whether they be Communists or not, who in the main are poor people.

I am not anti-Communist as a sociologist because the Communist proposals to combat poverty, hunger, illiteracy, and lack of housing and public services are effective and scientific.

I am not anti-Communist as a Christian, because I believe that anti-Communism condemns the whole of Communism, without acknowledging that there is some justice in its cause, as well as injustice. By condemning the whole we condemn the just and the unjust, and this is anti-Christian.

I am not anti-Communist as a priest because, whether the Communists realize it or not, there are within their ranks some authentic Christians. If they are working in good faith, they might well be the recipients of sanctifying grace. Should this be true, and should they love their neighbor, they would be saved. My role as a priest, even though I am not exercising its prerogatives externally, is to lead all men to God. The most effective way to do this is to get men to serve the people in keeping with their conscience.

I do not intend to proselitize among the Communists and to try to get them to accept the dogma and teachings of the Catholic Church. I do want all men to act in accordance with their conscience, to look in earnest for the truth, and to love their neighbor effectively.

The Communists must be fully aware of the fact that I will not join their ranks, that I am not nor will I ever be a Communist, either as a Colombian, as a sociologist, as a Christian, or as a priest.

Yet I am disposed to fight with them for common objectives: against the oligarchy and the domination of the United States, and for the takeover of power by the popular class.

I do not want public opinion to identify me with the Communists. This is why in all my public appearances I have wanted to be surrounded not only by the Communists but by all revolutionaries, be they independent or followers of other movements.

It matters little that the press is bent on depicting me as a Communist. I prefer to follow my conscience, rather than give in to the pressures of the oligarchy. I prefer to follow the directives of the Pontiffs of the Church rather than those of the pontiffs of our ruling class. John XXIII authorized me to march in unity of action with the Communists when he wrote the following lines in his encyclical "Pacem in Terris."

76

It must be borne in mind, furthermore, that neither can false philosophical teachings regarding the nature, origin and destiny of the universe and of man be identified with historical movements that have economic, social, cultural or political ends, not even when these movements have originated from those teachings and have drawn and still draw inspiration therefrom.

This is so because the teachings, once they are drawn up and defined, remain always the same, while the movements, working in historical situations in constant evolution, cannot be influenced by these latter and cannot avoid, therefore, being subject to changes, even of a profound nature. Besides, who can deny that those movements, in so far as they conform to the dictates of right reason and are interpreters of the lawful aspirations of the human person, contain elements that are positive and deserving of approval?

It can happen, then, that a drawing nearer together or a meeting for the attainment of some practical end, which was formerly deemed inopportune or unproductive, might now or in the future be considered opportune and useful.

But to decide whether this moment has arrived and also to lay down the ways and degrees in which work in common might be possible for the achievement of economic, social, cultural and political ends which are

honorable and useful, are problems which can
only be solved with the virtue of prudence,
which is the guiding light of the virtues that
regulate the moral life, both individual and
social.

Once the popular class assumes power, with the
help of all revolutionaries, then our people will be
ready to discuss the religious orientation they
should give their lives.

Poland is an example of how socialism can be established without destroying what is essential in
Christianity. As a Polish priest once said: 'As
Christians we have the obligation of contributing
to the construction of a socialist state so long as we
are allowed to adore God as we wish.'

September 2, 1965   *Camilo Torres*

MESSAGE TO THE MILITARY

After reflecting on the power of forty disciplined
and armed men against a multitude of four thousand persons in the city of Girardot, I have decided
to make an earnest call to the armed forces of Colombia, asking them to become fully conscious of
the historical moment we are living, so that they
will decide to plan, from this moment on, the ways
in which they will participate in the revolutionary
struggle.

On several occasions I have seen uniformed peasants and workers strike and persecute other peasants, workers, and students who, in fact, represent
the majority of Colombians. Neither among the
uniformed nor the officer corps did I ever find,

with but rare exceptions, members of the ruling class. Anyone who has thought about the contrast between the Colombian majorities clamoring for revolution and the small military minority repressing the people in order to protect a few privileged families, must wonder about the reasons which encourage members of the lower classes to persecute their comrades.

Economic advantages are not the answer. All the personnel of the armed forces are very badly paid. In general, military men are not allowed to pursue studies which might enable them to have a life apart from the army. When they are promoted to major they try to buy a home on a corner where they can set up a store which will give them an income after they are retired. I have seen generals and colonels getting jobs as physical education teachers in secondary schools, and as insurance brokers. The salaries of the personnel on active duty are low, but those of the retired are even lower. The latter don't receive any medical attention or economic advantage. Yet we know that one third of the national budget goes to the armed forces. Obviously, the money is not spent on salaries but rather on the materiel that is sold to us by the United States, on the maintenance of equipment, and on continuing the internal repression by which Colombians kill their own brothers.

It could be that the reason the military act the way they do is that they are committed to the laws, to the Constitution, and to the Fatherland. But the Colombian Fatherland is made up of men, and the majority of these suffer and do not enjoy power. The Constitution is constantly violated when the people are denied work, property, liberty, and a share in the exercise of power. For, after all, the Constitution does state that the people are responsible for decision-making in public affairs. The Constitution is violated when martial law is maintained long after the causes for its declaration have ceased to exist. The laws are violated when citizens are arrested without a warrant, when mail is retained, when citizens cannot walk in the streets, when telephones are tapped, and when lying is used the better to persecute revolutionaries.

Perhaps the military need clearer instruction on where the Fatherland, the Constitution, and the laws are to be found, so that they will not think that they can be equated with twenty-four families they currently protect, for whom they spill their blood and from whom they receive such pitiful remuneration.

Perhaps the principal reason why the military continue to support the oligarchy is the lack of other fields of human activity in Colombia. The military must understand that when the revolution triumphs the economy will be planned, and the schools and universities will be opened to all Colombians. Not only the present generation but its children as well will have the opportunity to get good jobs and to follow liberal careers. So long as the reactionary enemy remains, an army will exist not for the defense of the privileged minorities but for the defense of the people. The sacrifices that will be made then will be made to construct the Fatherland, not to destroy it.

The honor of the armed forces will no longer be tied to the whims of the oligarchy and of the lackeys that the armed forces might have at their service. No longer will three-sun generals be stripped of their rank for talking about structural reforms and pressure groups. No longer will we see generals with middle class origins being fired for engaging in contraband and causing public scandals, while the elite of the upper class or those related to the Colombian oligarchy profit from contraband without being discovered. And the contraband of the latter goes directly against the interests of the country and national sovereignty.

Soldiers: the United Front promises to organize and give unity to the popular class in its struggle for the takeover of power. Do not stay away from the battlefield where we will inflict a mortal blow to that oligarchy which oppresses all Colombians, which oppresses you as it does all of us.

Camilo Torres

September 9, 1965

MESSAGE TO THE NON-ALIGNED

The corrupt and lax symptoms of the National Front are common to those of all worn out regimes in their last agonizing moments. The leaders drown in parties and bacchanals the uneasiness which popular ferment causes them, and devote their political activity to deals worked out in coteries, to internecine struggles among outdated and unpopular leaders. The people are no longer interested in the quarrels of the Llerases, the Gomezes, the Ospinas, and the Santos, as well as of other members of our feudal aristocracy.

The people are hungry; they are unhappy. They have decided to unite and organize themselves. But above all, the people are determined to take power.

In the elections of the past, the oligarchy still had no need to invent votes. If we allow the next elections to take place, the oligarchy will have to invent many votes.

The abstainers were the majority in the electorate. Seventy per cent of the Colombians did not vote. Anyone who has even the slightest knowledge of the Colombian people, anyone who has attended the popular rallies before the elections, must have been convinced that the abstainers were opponents of the National Front and of the oligarchy.

In general the abstainers are revolutionaries who are not organized in political groups. Though it is true, thanks to the revolutionary and anti-sectarian spirit which has been revealed by political groups which have joined the United Front, that the adherence of these groups to the Front has gained for them a greater number of supporters, the majority of Colombians have joined the United Front without becoming members of the existing political groups. The latter must understand that the principal task of the United Front must be the organization of the non-aligned.

The organization of the non-aligned must be done from the bottom to the top, using the people's own leaders, with provision made for strong, but not caudillistic, leadership. At present the principal link among them is the platform of the United Front of the People which I proposed to the Colombian popular class. It is possible that my name is still too important within this group, and in the initial stage it might well be that my name will serve to stimulate revolutionary agitation and organization. But it would be infantile to repeat the same errors of other revolutionary movements which have failed in the past. We have seen how the oligarchy assassinated Jorge Eliecer Gaitan. We have seen how the reaction of the people at the time was not to reorganize themselves around revolutionary leaders. Rather they turned to the heads of the oligarchy and carried these men, who sold out the revolutionary movement, to the presidential palace. We saw how a disorganized people tried to do battle with the enemy in those cities where he was strongest. A disconcerted people fell prey to the madness of arson and robbery instead of returning to the camps where the enemy was weakest and where the revolutionaries could count on greater resources.

We are betting on a race with the oligarchy. It is possible that the oligarchy will assassinate me before I have a chance to give solid organization to the non-aligned. I think it would be too dull of them to imprison me or to wage a verbal battle against me. This is why I think it will be assassination. What is important, then, is that the Colombian people have the watch-word before this comes to pass.

First, they must go out to the rural areas and not fight the battle in the cities.

Second, they must not take any offensive action so long as there is no rural organization capable of maintaining it.

Above all it is necessary that the non-aligned realize the gravity of the moment and their historic responsibility. Every minute we lose in organization is a minute of advantage we give to the oligarchy.

Massive demonstrations and revolutionary enthusiasm and agitation are useful insofar as they are reflected immediately in a solid organization at the grassroots.

It is necessary that every peasant, every worker, and every revolutionary feel responsible to form a commando of the United Front with some of his friends or colleagues, without expecting directives and orders.

They must meet to:

1) Discuss and divulge the platform of the United Front.

2) Distribute and finance the periodical 'United Front.'

3) Comply with the immediate watchwords for action.

4) Coordinate their activities with those of other grassroots commandos to create additional

commandos in districts, neighborhoods, factories, schools and universities, municipalities, regions, and departments.

5) Prepare the delegates for the great national convention of the people to be held December 11-12, 1965.

The popular manifestation scheduled for 5 p.m. on October 10 at the Plaza Bolivar will be the opportunity for the non-aligned to present themselves organized in commandos and work-groups. During this manifestation the people of Colombia, especially those of Bogota, will denounce the state of siege and all its repressive consequences which have so affected them, namely, verbal battles, the persecution of unions and of leaders of the opposition, the new taxes, the last devaluation, etc.

Electoral abstention in itself is not an instrument for revolutionary combat. It must be accompanied by an organization, and by an active and belligerent discipline. The non-aligned and the revolutionaries without a party will have to transform themselves from an amorphous and weak mass into a battering ram which will not cease to attack the system until it is totally destroyed.

September 16, 1965   *Camilo Torres*

MESSAGE TO THE UNION WORKERS

Few groups in Colombia have the tradition of struggle and organization that the workers do, especially the urban laborers.

In spite of the fact that industry in Colombia was not of national importance until 1939, unionism, both urban and rural, already had a tradition of struggle prior to this date.

The uprisings of the banana workers give witness to this struggle. The government of Alfonso Lopez marked a fundamental stage in labor organization and Colombian union battling. Unionism arose as a belligerent and independent force. Very soon, however, it began to lose strength, because of the infiltration of paternalistic and imperialistic elements, and of strikebreakers sold out to reactionary governments. Our ruling class was successful in dividing our working class. After weakening it with religious and political pretexts, as it had weakened the popular class, it decided to purge "Communist" elements from the workers at the Congress of Cartagena. In other words, what it sought to do was to discard all elements which were not subject to North American or national patronship.

Nevertheless, the pressure of the system touched all workers alike. The movement begun by Gaitan consolidated a class consciousness which nineteen years of violence unleashed by the establishment has not been able to erase. The mercenary leaders, who have sold out to the oligarchy, are increasingly more prominent. Consequently, their procedures are progressively more arbitrary and violent as they struggle to remain in power.

The National Front accelerates the social struggle in Colombia by becoming the first class party in the country, a party of the privileged class, which consolidates the union of the oppressors against the oppressed. It defies the popular class to create what Jose Antonio Galan called 'The union of the oppressed against the oppressors.'

The government of the National Front has effected three devaluations, has increased public and military expenditure by 200%, and has tried to remedy the fiscal bankruptcy by levying a sales and gasoline tax on the people. The nation-wide strike of January 25 is the culmination of a social ferment which was sold out to the oligarchies. . . . But the system is so disintegrated and corrupt that not even the parliamentary political machinery could function in their favor.

Recourse was taken in the installation of a dictatorship. A state of siege was declared, taking advantage of a student strike. The state of siege continues, in violation of the Constitution, to make possible legislation on economic matters, and to allow the establishment to practice demagoguery with the workers. What is most grave about the present system is that not only the workers but the oligarchy too are unhappy. And when the oligarchy is unhappy the possibility of a coup d'etat is imminent.

When the political team fails the oligarchy alternates it with the military team. Should a military government take power now, it would probably awaken hopes by passing demagogic measures. But in recent times the Colombian people have unanimously cried for revolution. Yet they still lack a well-formed conscience and an adequate organization to resist the fraud which will be prevalent in the demagogic measures that will be passed after the fall of the hated government of the National Front.

An endless series of legal and illegal strikes has begun in our country. All those struggles or immediate triumphs strengthen the revolutionary struggle because they unify, organize, and consolidate the conscience of Colombian labor. The labor base of all the union offices is unified, as are many of the leaders, around the platform of the United Front of the People. The workers and students together constitute the bastion which will confront the new wiles of the oligarchy. All in all, the workers must decide to use their limited financial resources and their indisputable organizational talents in the revolutionary struggle and in the organization of the rest of the Colombian popular class.

It has been said that the unionists are the oligarchs of the popular class. I do not believe this is so. The oligarchy is decidedly inclined toward exploitation. The unionists, on the other hand, even those who work for monopolistic businesses and who, therefore, enjoy a measure of privilege which goes along with these firms, have assumed in many cases a frankly revolutionary spirit bent on recovering what is rightfully theirs.

It is imperative, in this crucial moment of our history, that the Colombian working class dedicate all its efforts to unify and organize the Colombian popular class for the final take-over of power.

Let not any partial struggle for immediate gains make us forget that the total and definitive vindication of the workers cannot take place other than as a consequence of the take-over of power by the majorities, by the Colombian popular class.

On the unity, the organization, and the capacity to fight with what we have so far recovered depend the unity, the organization, and the struggle for the ultimate triumph.

The same union leaders who are afraid of publicizing the platform of the United Front are afraid of unity because they know that a united and organized working class would make them pay dearly for having sold out to the ruling classes, both national and foreign.

The working class, like the Colombian people, has been superior to many of its leaders. When the working class is unified at the base it will exert the necessary pressure so that the leaders who are opposed to the union and to the revolution can be thrown out by a people now bent on taking power.

September 25, 1965   *Camilo Torres*

MESSAGE TO THE PEASANTS

According to the recent census the rural population has diminished. However, the census includes in the urban sectors all towns of more than 1,500 inhabitants. In reality this is not so. We can say that the majority of the Colombian population is rural.

In addition to their number, it is important to point out that the largest contribution to the national income is made by the peasants. Ninety per cent of the exports are agricultural (coffee, bananas, tobacco, sugar). Without agriculture, we could not import the machines nor the food we need. Unfortunately, the contribution of the peasants, like everything else in the system, can be enjoyed only by a few. Those who control the Federations (of coffee, cotton, tobacco and banana growers), the United Fruit Company and those who manage the banks (especially the Bank of the Republic), concentrate all the gains in their hands. The gains which the government makes use of are spent on "operation," in other words, in paying employees (whose jobs have been duplicated for political reasons), and to buy obsolete arms to kill the peasants who have contributed money to pay for them in the first place.

The contrast between the economic and social importance of the peasants, and the treatment they receive from the existing system, is manifestly scandalous. Violence has been carried out primarily by the peasants, though the government was responsible for initiating it. Since 1947 the police have been involved in violence and since 1948 the army, too.

The Liberal oligarchies paid the Liberal peasants

and the Conservative oligarchies paid the Conservative peasants so that the peasants would kill one another. The oligarchs themselves received not a scratch. When the oligarchy no longer needed them it denounced them as bandits, it hunted them like beasts and then, when it assassinated them, it published the photographs of their bodies on the front page of the great press saying that it had obtained a victory in the name of peace, justice and legality.

That violence, directed by the government and financed by the oligarchy, taught the peasants many lessons: above all it taught them to recognize in the oligarchy their greatest enemy. It taught them to flee at first, later to defend themselves, and finally to attack in order to obtain what the oligarchy obtained by violence: estates, harvests, livestock, power. These things the system did not give them. On the contrary, the peasants got the lowest salaries, the least number of schools, the worst houses, and the fewest possibilities to progress.

When the most notorious guerrilla leaders were killed, the rural areas remained under the control of the agricultural laborers themselves.

The repressive policy of the United States, imposed upon the Colombian government, could not allow the existence of 'suspicious' zones even though these might be pacific. The army needed to enhance its importance, to show that this was necessary, and to increase its budget.

The government says that the peasants started

the violence. The peasants say it was the government. French *intellectuals of all ideological currents* assert, after careful investigation, that the peasants are right.

I want to defy the government to ask the United Nations, if it dares, to send a fact-finding team made up of neutral nations (such as Egypt, India, or Chile) to investigate the happenings in Marquetalia, Pato, Guayabero and Rio Chiquito.

We know that there is great similarity between the landing of the marines in Santo Domingo and the landings of the Colombian army, directed by the United States military mission, in the 'independent republics.'

These landings will continue. Yesterday in Rio Chiquito, tomorrow in Sumapaz, day-after-tomorrow in Ariari and the Llanos. The army begins with civil-military action and ends with bombings. It starts by extracting molars and ends by pumping in bullets. The peasants already know that the military carry bread in the hand they put forward and a dagger in the one they hold back. The 'dependent republic' of Colombia will continue to obey the North Americans so that it will destroy with blood and fire the other republics of independent Colombians. This is what the United States Congress has decreed. Our peasants already know what to expect. They already know what they must prepare for. They are not plunging into an adventure but neither are they fleeing from a fight. By declaring martial law the oligarchy has already removed the people from the public *plazas*. It is also using its machine guns in remote quarters such as Medellin. When it makes life in the city impossible for us we will have to go to the country. And from the country we will not be able to plunge into the sea. There we will have to resist. And for this reason the peasantry must be prepared. This can be done immediately by organizing commandos of the United Front into groups of from five to ten persons, securing areas where traitors have sold out the cause of the people. Food and clothing deposits must be set up, in order to prepare for the prolonged struggle. We must remember not to allow ourselves to be provoked or to resist when such actions could spell disaster for the people.

The actions of the oligarchy will convince the peasants that they must support the revolutionary forces. Why hasn't the guerrilla in Simacota been suppressed? The answer is only because of the support of the peasants.

When the oligarchy leaves us no alternative, the peasants will have to provide refuge for the urban, labor, and student revolutionaries.

For the moment they must unify and organize to be able to receive us and begin the last long struggle.   *Camilo Torres*

October 7, 1965

MESSAGE TO THE WOMEN

The Colombian women, like women in all underdeveloped countries, have always occupied an inferior position with respect to men and the society. This situation varies according to the standard of living of the people.

Within the popular class, the woman has many duties of a material nature and almost none of a spiritual nature. The highest degree of illiteracy is found among the women of the popular class. They must work very hard in the hidden, but often quite arduous, domestic tasks (kitchen-gardens, pigs, chickens, dogs, etc.) to say nothing of the difficulties and responsibilities of motherhood.

The woman of the working class enjoys no social or legal protection. When, in a country like ours, a man is harassed by misery, unemployment, and the weighty responsibilities of a numerous family, he sometimes takes refuge, mistakenly, in vices: he abandons the home and his wife must assume the responsibilities. How often we see the homes of working parents locked during the day and filled with half-naked and hungry children awaiting the return of their mother from her daily job.

The woman of the middle class is also exploited by the masters. It is possible that within this class the relations with the husband are on a more equal basis. Nevertheless, these families could not survive if the woman did not work, and we know that the woman who works, be she an office-worker or an employee, suffers all kinds of exploitation and pressures from her boss.

The woman of the upper class must while away the time playing cards and attending social gatherings to kill the boredom which comes from the lack of opportunities to pursue an intellectual or professional life. Marital fidelity is demanded only of the woman. The sanctions are swift for any transgressions in this regard. In spite of the fact that the law establishes the equality of rights and duties, in reality this law is but a dead letter.

As regards politics, to date the men of the popular class have been subjected to the whims of the oligarchy. Electoral abstention has been the first cry of rebellion of a whole class which is fed up with the fictions of the ruling class.

Other symptoms of organization and unification already exist among the discontent. Yet the oligarchy, as an octopus, has already extended its tentacles to entangle the Colombian women. The men of the oligarchy gave the women the vote to be able to continue to use them as instruments.

Nevertheless, the Colombian woman has values as a human person and is not simply an instrument. The Colombian woman realizes that she is exploited not only by the society, as are the majority of Colombians, but by the men. The Colombian woman is disciplined for the struggle; she has shown generosity in giving of herself to others, and has great resistance to physical pain. The Colombian woman, like all women, has more feeling, more sensitivity, and more intuition. All these qualities must be magnified and put to the service of a revolutionary ideal which must become the ideal of the women. They must not be put to the service of the oligarchy or of the men as such.

In fact, it would not be exaggerated to say that the women, because of their greater intuition, have been able to see through the electoral slips of paper and the partisan struggles which have taken such a hold on the men. The Colombian woman has not yet fallen prey to the selfish desire for power. The oligarchs want to tempt her in this respect, but they do not realize that if it is true that the Colombians have a "native suspicion," the women have it ten times worse. The women know very well that the vote is but a new form of exploitation being used by the oligarchy. This is one reason why they attend public meetings to give expression to even greater and more patriotic ideals. The Colombian woman is preparing for the revolution. She has been and she will continue to be the mainstay of the revolutionary man. She must be at the heart of the revolution. If each revolutionary man had a wife at home who knew how to encourage him, how to understand him, and how to help him, we would have many more men committed to the struggle. After the revolution the women will come to realize that the equality of rights and obligations will no longer be a dead letter. Rather equality will be a reality which the women themselves, as a popular and revolutionary force, will be able to guarantee.

The problems of divorce and birth control, which the Colombian woman believes can be resolved within a conformist and oppressive system, in reality can only be resolved by a system which respects freedom of conscience and individual, familial, and social rights. These problems will not be resolved until there is a State which is truly autonomous, while at the same time being respectful of the ecclesiastical hierarchy.

The Colombian woman is sufficiently generous to be able to solve her personal problems within the framework of a larger ideal, where these problems will be resolved without overlooking the needs of others.

This ideal will not become a reality without a genuine revolution in Colombia.

Camilo Torres

Bogota, October, 1965.

MESSAGE TO THE STUDENTS

The students are a privileged group in all underdeveloped countries. At a very high cost the poor nations support the graduates of their schools and universities. In Colombia, where there are so many private schools and universities, economic status has become the determining factor in education. In a country where sixty per cent are illiterate, eight per cent have a Bachelor's degree, and one per cent are professionals, the students are among the very few groups who can analyze the Colombian situation, compare it with that of other countries, and offer possible solutions.

In addition, the university and high school students who enjoy freedom of speech have two privileges: to be able to rise in the social ladder by ascending the academic one; and to be able to express their dissatisfaction without endangering their academic career. These advantages have enabled the students to play a decisive role in the Latin American revolution. Their action has been most effective particularly in the agitational phase of the revolution. In the organizational phase their role has been of secondary importance. In the actual battle, despite worthy exceptions, their role has been minor.

We know that agitation is important, but it is ineffective if it is not followed up by organization and a struggle for the takeover of power. One of the principal reasons why the students' contribution to the Revolution has been only transitory and superficial is the students' lack of involvement in the economic, familial, and personal struggle. Their dissatisfaction tends to be emotional (because of sentimentalism or frustration), or purely intellectual. This is one reason why their dissatisfaction tends to die down at the end of their university years. The rebellious student becomes a bourgeois professional who, in order to buy the symbols of prestige of the bourgeoisie, sells his conscience in exchange for a large salary.

These circumstances could represent a serious threat to a mature and responsible answer on the part of the students to the historic moment Colombia is living through at present. The economic and political crisis is being felt especially by the workers and peasants. The students, who in general are isolated from these groups, can afford to engage in purely superficial or speculative revolutionary activity. This very lack of contact could cause the students to betray their historic vocation. When the country needs their total commitment, they could be victims of nothing but verbiage and good intentions. When the masses demand daily and constant dedication, the students could be content with shouting, rock-hurling, and sporadic manifestations. When the popular class begs for effective, disciplined, and responsible action the students could answer with vain promises or with excuses.

It is essential that the revolutionary conviction of each student be so engrained that he accept it in its totality, even to the utlimate consquences. Poverty and persecution must not be sought after. But, given the present situation, they are the logical consequences of a battle to the end against the existing structures. Under the present system, they are the signs which give authenticity to a revolutionary life. The same conviction should make the students share in the economic and social hardships of the workers and peasants. Only then does the commitment to revolution pass from theory to practice. If it is total it is irreversible: the professional will not be able to turn back without a flagrant betrayal of his conscience, of his people, and of his historic vocation.

I do not want to be dogmatic about the critical revolutionary moment we are living. I only wish to exhort the students to make contact with the real sources of information so that they will know when the real moment arrives, what their responsibility is, and consequently, what their answer should be. Personally, I believe we are moving swiftly toward the zero hour of the Colombian revolution. But this no one will know with certainty without consulting the workers and peasants. If students are able "to enter the popular class," without paternalism, and with the attitude of wanting to learn rather than teach, they will be able to judge objectively the historic moment.

It would be very unfortunate if for any reason the Colombian students, who have been the spark of the revolution, were unable to participate in it because they lacked information or were somehow superficial, egotistic, irresponsible or fearful.

We hope that the students will be able to answer the call of their country in this transcendental moment of its history. To do this, they must be disposed to listen to the call and to answer it with boundless generosity.   *Camilo Torres*

October 21, 1965

MESSAGE TO THE UNEMPLOYED

Although it is true that in all capitalist countries, including the most developed ones such as the United States, there exists a large percentage of unemployed, it must be emphasized that in the underdeveloped countries the percentage is even greater. The lack of work for millions of men and women is, precisely, one of the characteristics of the underdeveloped countries. In a rich country like Colombia, the oligarchy has been unable to create a sufficient number of industries to give work to the thousands of Colombians who every year reach the age of employment and who want to be useful members of society.

100

The oligarchy neither wants to, nor is it able to, open new sources of work. It does not want to because it thinks of itself more than of the country. It prefers to send its money to Canada or Switzerland rather than to invest it in Colombia. It is an oligarchy which is well aware of the sufferings it has caused the people, and because of this it is afraid, afraid especially of the Revolution. This is why it prefers to take its money out of the country rather than to invest it in new industries. It prefers to invest it in luxurious clubs and to spend it sumptuously rather than to invest it in new factories. It is not interested in creating new problems for itself by having to compete for the market with North American firms. Nor does it have the imagination or drive to look for technical and economic assistance in countries other than the United States for help in industrializing our country. It is a conformist oligarchy which was "born tired," and which has always thought more of itself and its foreign associates than of the real needs of the Colombian people.

But even if the oligarchy wanted to industrialize Colombia it would not be able to do so. Its North American associates would not permit this. We all know that there are many businesses which seem to be Colombian, though in reality they are more North American. Examples of these are Avianca, Peldar, Icollantas, Croydon, etc. We all know that our economy depends on the sale of coffee which goes principally to the United States and on the economic aid we get from the United States. We all know that ours is a beggar's state which depends on the crumbs that the North Americans might want to give us. We all know too that the North Americans themselves do not want us to industrialize. The help they give us goes to construct some little schools, a pilot community, or perhaps a few latrines, but they will never help us establish new factories for heavy machinery, factories which in turn will cause the creation of other factories which will then open up new job possibilities. What the United States is interested in is having countries which will supply it with cheap raw materials—both mineral and agricultural—and to which it can in turn sell expensive cars, machinery, and all the products of its industry which the underdeveloped countries need. The United States dominates our economy; our oligarchy is very happy to be its agent and servant.

This is why the unemployed are the ones who suffer most from the consequences of our underdevelopment. The misery of their homes, the anguish of not being able to take to their homes the necessary goods, of not being able to pay the rent, of not being able to educate their children, all these pressures are building up in the unemployed and showing them the need for a definitive struggle against the system. They are more aware than anyone else that they are not poor because they do not want to work, but because there is no place for them to work. They know that it is not the people who are lazy but the oligarchy, which is now "owner" of the sources of work and of the State, which does nothing to solve the real problems of the country. These

102

are the reasons why the unemployed should be at the head of the struggle to take power away from the minority and give it to the majority. They should be the first to understand that the people must be organized, because they are suffering the weight of the system. They must be the first to realize that so long as the people do not truly govern it will be impossible to solve the problems of our economy and, consequently, the problems of all the Colombian homes that today are affected by unemployment.

What is most grave is that this acute state of chronic unemployment seems to have no solution. On the contrary, every day the problem is more aggravated. In the Ministry of Work there are several hundred petitions of businesses requesting authorization to license personnel. There are many others which license personnel without authorization. Daily we learn of new cases of mass dismissals, and we know many small industries are forced to go out of business because of the rise in value of the dollar which causes a dramatic rise in the cost of raw materials.

Moreover, hundreds of thousands of persons have been displaced from rural to urban centers because of the violence which the oligarchy unleashed against our peasants. The latter must understand that the solutions to their problems will not come from their own executioners, from those who initiated the violence, from those who have the country mortgaged, from those who are responsible for the prevailing misery. Rather, the solution must come from the majority, one of whose most important sectors numerically is that of the unemployed.

Every day the crisis grows more acute. Because of its narrow, egotistical, and anti-national posture the oligarchy adds daily to the ranks of the revolutionaries. When a man or a woman has nothing to lose—not even a job with a meager salary—participation in the struggle could mean a total gain and the loss only of one's chains. When this is the situation of a whole people it means that the hour of liberation is closer every minute.

This is the struggle of all the people against a handful of oppressors whose only support are arms and foreign aid. In that struggle the people will be victorious because no force is able to stop the triumph of a united people fighting for their rights, inspired by noble and generous ideals. The people prefer to fight to gain power once and for all rather than die of hunger and cold, and suffer more misery and humiliations. The oligarchy has obliged them to act so. The oligarchy has challenged our people and we have accepted that challenge.

Camilo Torres

October 28, 1965

MESSAGE TO THE UNITED FRONT OF THE PEOPLE

Two conditions have made it possible for the United Front of the Colombian People to have the extension and vitality it has after only five months of life. First, our decision to carry the struggle on to the very end no matter what the cost until the people take over the power. Second, our insistence on unity in the platform, stressing those points which unite us, and overlooking those which do not. These two characteristics have enticed many revolutionaries who heretofore acted in isolation to join forces and avoid a waste of energy by becoming members of, and working for the revolution within the United Front, thus adding to the strength of the existing organizations.

This was not easy to accomplish nor has it been fully realized. It is true that we have commandos in all the large cities of the country and in some of the smaller ones. It is also true that our weekly continues to be published and that it has considerable circulation. But this is not enough. Unfortunately, in many cases the Colombian revolutionaries still do not understand the importance of unity. They allow themselves to be distracted by discussions which could be important, but which at present cannot be justified in light of the demand of the majority for unity and action. In many cases the revolutionaries think more of their personal problems than of the Revolution, and they place their personal affairs above those of the group.

What is even more grave is that in many cases not even important theoretical differences exist. Only petty grudges inherited from old disputes between groups and even between persons. But if we analyze the obligations which as revolutionaries we have before the people, if we realize the immensity of the task before us, if we are successful in stripping ourselves of egotism and sectarianism, we shall see how these little conflicts shrink and lose their importance.

This is why I believe that one of the most important tasks of the non-aligned is to unite all the revolutionaries around a Platform, avoiding, in so far as possible, the emergence of problems which would divide rather than unite persons, parties, or groups. This is one of the greater responsibilities of the non-aligned. They must search constantly for elements of unification and try to avoid all situations which lead to conflict. We must never forget that we are interested in the sum total of our efforts, not in their diminution. This is why we have declared a war to the death against all that is anti-revolutionary, and why we have said that we are friends of ALL revolutionaries, no matter where they come from.

We are not going to underestimate or misuse the help that each revolutionary can give and would like to give to the revolution. We believe that the United Front must be a recipient to which all the people, but especially the revolutionaries, can give what they have to give. At times the small help of a poor but dedicated revolutionary could be of far greater value than the interested help devoid of convictions given by other people.

In any event, we can already say that we have a measure of organization throughout the country. Even though it is not as extended or as disciplined as we would like it to be, we can feel satisfied that we have completed a first stage, and that all the agitation that has accompanied my trips and the publication of the periodical, have had their first fruits. But now the organization is facing a new stage—that of strengthening and solidifying our gains to date. We cannot allow the task of organization to become stagnant, because we are convinced that every minute we lose now we will have to pay doubly when we have to organize the people while at the same time suffering the implacable persecution that the oligarchy will unleash against us. Within this plan, preparation of the convention for the beginning of next year will be of great importance inasmuch as it will constitute a decisive step.

The United Front of the People must never disappear under any circumstances. No matter how many pressures are exerted against us and no matter how many of us are taken prisoners, the United Front must continue to function. Even though I myself might be obliged at a given moment to seek refuge in a safe place in order to continue the struggle, the legal battle must not cease. We will continue to publish the periodical until it is shut down. But even if this happens, we will publish another. For we must do all that is possible to have the legal organ of the United Front constantly circulating throughout the country. And this is the responsibility not only of those who write for it, but also of those who distribute it and who buy it.

We state the above because we have never had any illusions, nor have we spoken of them to the popular class. I think that the minority class will wage a general war of extermination against all the people, a war which it has already started in some regions of the country. Consequently, I believe that the United Front must prepare itself, redoubling its efforts to be able to resist the attack of the oligarchy. And as we propose not only to resist but to be victorious, and as what we want is not to leave the oligarchy alone so that it can leave us alone with our misery, but on the contrary we want to decide our destiny once and for all by confronting the minority in an all out struggle, we feel, therefore, that the United Front must be strengthened more and more every day.

This is why we stress the need for unity among the revolutionaries. We know that the stages of change that are coming upon us will be infinitely more difficult than those we have lived through so far. We realize that if we do not struggle together the cost in suffering to the people will be very great, and in this sense, the gains to the revolutionary cause will be diminished. If this should happen we, the revolutionaries, would be responsible for not being able to put the interests of the people above our own differences.

Our people are courageous. Our people are not afraid of confronting the exploiting minority, because they have behind them years of suffering without hope. In the thesis of the United Front our people have seen a hope. This is why it would be a crime on our part to betray them again. We must learn from the people and feel stimulated by their example and their enthusiasm for the struggle. United the people are invincible. They are capable of conquering whatever they confront, no matter how many arms or how much money the enemy might have.

Let us, then, make a great effort so that our organization will be the revolutionary movement the people have been waiting for, so that the Christians, the Marxists, the non-aligned, the members of the MRL, of the ANAPO, the Liberals, the Conservatives, and all the poor of Colombia find in it an effective means of confronting the oligarchy. The tactical differences which separate us at present do not matter. By our example we must convince all of the need for unity and of the possibility of attaining our final objective: the takeover of power by the people, no matter what the cost.

November 25, 1965   *Camilo Torres*

MESSAGE TO THE POLITICAL PRISONERS

The people of Colombia must understand that the minority which controls power today will not give it up without a struggle. We must recall how difficult was the fight against the Spaniards in the nineteenth century, and the many hardships that the revolutionaries had to endure during that period. It could be said that a good test as to whether or not a person or organization is revolutionary is the posture adopted by the oligarchy. The more revolutionary they are the more the oligarchy will persecute them. The foreigners and the oligarchy know very well who really wants to take power from them to give it to the people, and who is interested only in personal or other advantages.

The oligarchy, therefore, knows very well who are its enemies, and those it persecutes relentlessly. This is why Narino, for example, who fought with gun in hand and who was not interested in obtaining privileges for the wealthy creoles, but rather in improving the lot of the people, had to spend many years in jail, persecuted not only by the Spaniards, but also by many "great leaders" of the Independence Movement who belonged to the existing oligarchy, and whose descendents are the "great leaders" of today.

This is why the oligarchy will persecute us every day with greater ferocity. When it realizes that we are ready to carry our struggle to its ultimate consequences in order to take over power for the people, that minority which did not vacillate in opening the country to violence, in selling our sovereignty to foreign powers, in converting our soldiers into an army which occupies its own fatherland, that minority whose hand did not tremble when it assassinated popular leaders, will unleash against the United Front of the People and against all popular organizations the force of its repressive machinery.

This must not surprise us nor must it scare us. The oligarchy has a dual moral code which it uses to condemn revolutionary violence while it assassinates and jails the defenders and representatives of the popular class. It is the same double standard that the United States has: while it talks of peace it is bombing Viet Nam and landing in Santo Domingo. This is why the oligarchy and the United

States understand one another. But as we know that an entire people cannot be jailed, and that armed and organized peasants will not allow themselves to be thrown into the sea, we are not frightened by their repressive moves against us.

I have already said that it is a duty of the revolutionaries not to allow themselves to be assassinated. If we are persecuted in the cities we will go to the countryside, where we will be on equal terms with the envoys of the oligarchy. Unfortunately, not all the revolutionaries can or should take such an extreme measure. Many will undoubtedly be imprisoned by the oligarchical government and some could even be tortured by it. But the revolutionary who is imprisoned does not cease to be a valuable element in the struggle.

From his prison cell, the revolutionary must be an example of courage and decision, of a spirit of sacrifice and of loyalty to the Revolution. He must employ his time in studying and in preparing himself better to understand the justice of the revolutionary ideals, and to temper his ways for the day he regains his freedom. Moreover, the political prisoner must show the guards and the other prisoners that there is a profound difference between himself and the common criminal. The revolutionary must demand from his jailers treatment in keeping with his condition as a defender of the people. There is nothing more demoralizing for the enemy than our own courage and integrity. Rather than feeling shame for being imprisoned, the revolutionary must feel proud of the fear with which the oligarchy views him. He must feel proud of "suffering persecutions for the sake of justice."

The popular class must see in the imprisoned revolutionary a further stimulus to continue the struggle against the oligarchy. It must see in him a vanguard combatant deserving of much appreciation and support. Consequently, it must give him its solidarity by demanding his liberty, and by giving him food, money, clothing, books, information, etc. Nevertheless, the greatest help that popular organizations in general, and the revolutionaries in particular, can give to a prisoner, is to enhance his struggle. He must know that while he is behind bars, thousands upon thousands of men and women are fighting to make the revolution a reality; they are fighting to give him back his liberty. The best way to avoid that prisoners be taken from among the people is for the people to take over power.

It does not matter, then, that the oligarchy wishes to frighten the revolutionaries. It does not matter that the oligarchy betrays its "democratic" principles and turns judicial power over to the military to wash its hands and oblige the army to sin again in the eyes of the people, by condemning the revolutionaries with warlike language. Perhaps the military themselves will one day come to realize the hypocrisy and pharisaic behavior of our twenty-four millionaire families and of the unscrupulous politicians who serve as their mouthpieces. Insofar as we are concerned, nothing will make us stop in our struggle to organize the people and to be at its side when power is taken over, nothing—no matter what the cost. We can affirm this because it is a decision of the majority without whose support and active participation neither jail nor the hardships of the struggle would make any sense.

November, 1965   *Camilo Torres*

MESSAGE TO THE OLIGARCHY

To direct a message to those who neither want nor can understand it is very hard. Nevertheless, it is a duty, and an historical duty at that, in a moment when the Colombian oligarchy is bent on culminating its iniquity against the fatherland and against all Colombians.

During more than 150 years the economic caste —those few families who control almost all of Colombia's wealth—have usurped political power for their own good. They have used all types of cunning and deceit to preserve power while mocking the people.

They invented the division between Liberals and Conservatives. This division, which the people could not understand, served the purpose of spreading hatred within the popular class itself. Those ancestral hatreds transmitted from fathers to sons have served only the oligarchy. While the poor fight, the rich govern for their own good. The people did not understand the politics of the rich. But all the anger they felt for not being able to eat or to study, for feeling sick, homeless, landless, and without work—all this rancour the poor Liberals unleashed against the poor Conservatives, and the poor Conservatives against the poor Liberals. The oligarchs, who were responsible for the miserable condition of the poor, looked happily on the bull-fights from ringside as their wealth grew and their rule tightened. The only difference which arose between the Liberal oligarchs and the Conservative oligarchs was the problem of the division of the national budget and of public offices. The budget and public income were not enough to satisfy the Conservative and Liberal oligarchs together. This is why they fought to get to power: to liquidate their electoral debts by giving public posts to their wealthy supporters, and to divide the budget completely excluding their political opponents.

For forty years the Liberals held no offices. The same thing happened to the Conservatives for the next sixteen years. The political and religious differences had ceased. The fights among the oligarchs were strictly over public funds and posts. Meanwhile the people realized that their fight for the Conservative party or for the Liberal party resulted only in a deeper sinking into misery. The wealthy did not realize that the people were fed up with them. When Jorge Eliecer Gaitan appeared unfurling the flag of moral restoration for the Republic, he did so as much against the Liberal oligarchy as against the Conservative. Both oligarchies, therefore, were his antagonists. The Liberal oligarchy became *gaitanista* (partisans of Gaitan) after the Conservative oligarchy killed Gaitan in the streets of Bogota.

114

Once started on the road to violence to retain power, the oligarchy will not cease to use that violence. It allowed the Liberal and Conservative peasants to kill one another. When the aggression, hatred, and rancour of the poor spilled over into an all-out battle of Colombia's needy, the oligarchy was alarmed and fostered a military coup. But the military government did not adequately serve the interests of the oligarchy. It was then that the head of the Liberal oligarchy, Doctor Alberto Lleras Camargo, and the head of the Conservative oligarchy, Doctor Laureano Gomez, met to make an examination of conscience and came to this conclusion. 'Because of our fighting over the budget and bureaucratic spoils, we almost lost power for the oligarchy. Let us stop fighting and make a contract to divide the country as one divides an estate, in half, to be shared by the two oligarchies. Share and share alike will be a good working principle. In this way we will be able to form a new party—the party of the oligarchy.' This is how the National Front was born, the first class party, the party of the Colombian oligarchy.

Once again the people were mocked. They voted in the elections for the plebiscite, for Alberto Lleras, and for the National Front. Naturally, the result was worse. Now it was a united oligarchy governing against the people. The opposite of what the Colombians had hoped for came to pass. The National Front offered peace, but the peasants continued to be slaughtered. There were mass killings of sugar workers and of laborers in Santa Barbara.

The universities were invaded and the war budget was increased.

The National Front promised to remedy the financial situation: it doubled the foreign debt and effected (up to now) three devaluations, which mean greater misery for the Colombian people for several generations to come. The National Front promised an agrarian reform: it has dictated a law which guarantees the interests of the rich against the rights of the poor.

The National Front imposed on the country an inept presidential candidate: it was successful in obtaining the largest electoral abstention in the history of Colombia. Faced with this total failure, what is the oligarchy doing?

It takes recourse again to violence. It declares martial law. It legislates by decree. It sells the country to the United States. It meets in a luxurious hotel and decides on the next president. In salons it decides the future of the country. Its members are completely blind.

As a last cry of alarm I want to tell you:

Gentlemen of the oligarchy: the people no longer believe in you. They do not want to vote for you. They are fed up and desperate. They do not want to go to the elections you arrange for them. The people do not want Carlos nor Alberto Lleras, nor any of you. The people are suffering and they will do anything for relief. The people also know that you will do anything to save yourselves. This is why I ask you to be realistic: if you want to mock the people with new political deals you must know that they no longer have faith in you. You know that the fight will be carried out to its ultimate end. Existence has been so bitter that the people will stop at nothing. Unfortunately, the isolated, blind, and proud oligarchs seem not to want to realize that the revolution of the Colombian masses will not stop until the people have attained power.

Camilo Torres

December 9, 1965

POSSIBILITIES OF THE LEFT: LAST PROCLAMATION

Camilo Torres' statements to *Tercer Mundo*

What political characteristics predominate in Latin America?

The underdeveloped countries are characterized by the lack of industrialization. The latter means division of labor and the specialization and rationalization of human activity. What sociologists call primary relations, that is to say, face to face relations, those of greater intimacy and depth such as the family and friendship, constitute the predominant factor of social life in underdeveloped countries. Feeling and tradition rule the institutions, including the political. Sympathy for political currents does not stem from their programs as much as it does from the leadership of *caudillos*. Change in political affiliation, whether over generations or within the lifetime of an individual, is considered treason.

In countries which are classified as underde-

117

veloped but where political socialization is more evolved, we find a greater influence of ideology and rational elements. Nevertheless, this influence is felt in the normative plane of speculative theories. The underdeveloped countries which were colonized by the West, by cultures like the Spanish rooted in philosophy and Cartesian thinking, find it difficult to adopt empirical and positive values.

The Latin American countries in general, especially those which have had recently a limited immigration, and which have an indigenous or mixed population that is considerable, are faced with the problem of the co-existence of two cultures within one nationality: one which is typically Western, the patrimony of a minority and privileged class, descendants of the creoles; and the other of a syncretist nature in which indigenous elements mix (in varying proportions according to the countries) with Western elements.

The process of acculturation of the indigenous or *mestizo* (mixed blood) masses has followed the general laws. The material acculturation has been imposed while the non-material acculturation has had to be contented with imposing a few external forms without being successful at a total implantation of the content. We Latin Americans have received the juridical, political, religious, and economic institutions in their external forms alone (at least this is certainly true of the popular class) without having made our own the essence of these institutions.

118

When the creoles were confronted with the Independence Movement they were not able to give answers which were in keeping with the realities of the majority because they themselves had adopted the capitalist, bourgeois, and Western norms. Their solutions, therefore, were imported and totally irrelevant to the existing problems. A Movement as popular as that of the *Comuneros* in Colombia did not get the support of the creole bourgeoisie which was preoccupied with the translation and diffusion of the rights of man, which was of Western origin. Precious moments were lost in our struggle for independence in endless disputes over issues imported from abroad, such as federalism and centralism. The "Patria Boba," which incarnates the traditional ideological colonialism of our ruling class, has prolonged itself in less obvious ways down to our times. The predominant political attitudes in underdeveloped countries are sentimental, traditional, normative and speculative. There are also those which emanate from an ideological colonialism.

How do you see our political parties?

The political parties in Colombia manifest the attitudes mentioned above. In the beginning they copied the names and philosophies of the parties which had already been created in Europe. There were, however, from the start certain socio-economic principles which established a difference between Liberals and Conservatives. Today the ideological and religious differences have practi-

119

cally disappeared. The same is true of the socio-economic differences. From 1930 on partisan competition began to concentrate around the spoils from the national budget and the bureaucracy. The competition was aggravated by the increase in the budget resulting from the tax reform of 1936. The survival of the two traditional parties in Colombia must be explained by functional factors of some utility, both for the ruling class as well as for the popular class.

In any society membership in a group gives an individual a measure of personal security. This phenomenon is especially true in the societies of under-developed countries where the formal institutions for social and personal security are deficient. In Colombia, membership in one of the traditional parties is a way of acquiring security. If, in addition, the party is one of the few multi-class groups, not to say the only one, in which the common citizen finds means of identification with members of the highest social class, then the function of security is even more important. Add to this the sentimental and traditional factors with all they imply as regards social and psychological security and it will be easier to understand the importance that the political parties have for the popular class.

The ruling class was made up of a minority with conflicting philosophical and socio-economic interests which were not understood by the majority except in a most rudimentary way. When the conflicts within the ruling class disappeared, the political affiliation became a link, of the traditional type, with the popular class. When social and economic problems became paramount in the world and in Colombia, the Liberal-Conservative opposition was transformed into an opposition of classes.

By dividing Colombian society vertically, and by grouping the popular class into antagonistic factions based on tradition, the political parties prevented the creation of a class party. The absence of such a party assured the privileges of the ruling class and its predominance over the majority and popular class. Just as the political party in Colombia helps to give psychological security to the popular class, it helps, at the same time, to give socio-economic security to the ruling class.

Moreover, it should be noted that in almost all multi-class groups conformity is essential to upward social mobility. The exacting of conformity is the most effective means of control by a privileged minority over a destitute majority. This is why the lists of candidates for offices in Colombian organizations is made from above, imposed by the minority on the majority. Conformity is exacted ever more strictly as one ascends the political ladder.

The National Front is the result of the rationalization of a conflict—an emotional conflict centered around the budget and bureaucratic spoils. Violence and the administrative inefficiency of a military government, which were the consequences of the conflict, forced the leaders of the traditional parties to put aside their differences and sign a pact on the points of tension: the budget and the bureaucracy. Alternation and sharing of offices were an instrument of double effect: they formalized the contract for distribution of power and they guaranteed continuity in the division of the popular class along traditional and sentimental lines. These objectives were attained in short order. Yet the National Front, which was the first class party in Colombia and as such was responsible for a transcendental event in the country's political history, by its very existence forced the creation of an opposition class party: the party of the popular class.

What do you think of our progressive movements?

The leftist groups in Colombia have been conditioned by the political ideologies prevalent in underdeveloped countries. Many times our progressive leaders adhere to such ideologies for altruistic motives which can be identified with those of the Utopian socialists, and which have no scientific basis or rationally established tactics.

Traditionalism is manifested in them not by action but by reaction. Although scientifically that which is traditional might seem to be applicable, in reality it is often rejected because of resentment. The normative and speculative nature of our leaders results in their emphasizing theoretical pronouncements rather than offering practical solutions for our socio-economic problems. This orientation is closely linked to the ideological colonialism of our left. Slogans and cliches are taken over. A special revolutionary jargon is used. Colombian problems are given prefabricated solutions elabo-

122

rated abroad. Public manifestations are held in sympathy with the oppressed of the world, while ignoring the oppressed at home. Sentimentalism is translated into personalist caudillism and frustration. While the all-powerful minority ruling class unites to defend its interests, the leaders of the left attack one another, causing dismay within the popular class. In fact they represent the most authentic voice of traditionalism, sentimentalism, speculation, and ideological colonialism in Colombian politics.

Are there possibilities for popular integration?

The popular class in Colombia has been more successful in detaching itself from the ideological currents that predominate in underdeveloped countries than have the leaders of the left. Several historical circumstances have fostered the maturing of the popular class in its political attitudes and conceptions. The violence which has plagued Colombia put an end to the social isolation of the popular class and unleashed a conflict between the peasantry and the ruling class. It meant a break with our traditional, sentimental values, and gave us a more empirical and positive conception of our problems and those of our country. It was the beginning of the formation of class consciousness.

The National Front polarized the discontent not only with an individual, a government, or a party, but with a whole system and with a class. It was official and private programs for communal action, technical assistance given through the agrarian re-

123

form, and other similar projects which awakened class consciousness and pointed more forcefully to the needs. It also fostered a sense of security among popular groups. Labor and agrarian communities are recognizing the value of initiative and organization.

The popular class seems to be disillusioned with the democratic electoral system and this is why it stays away from the polls. It does not feel adequately represented by the leaders of the left who seem to be taken up with foreign ideologies and egotistical interests. More and more the popular class has confidence only in itself and increasingly distrusts elements of the other classes.

It is imperative that the intellectuals who are concerned with the good of the popular class realize their responsibility in the historic political and social moment we are experiencing. The people need concrete objectives for the social and economic development of the country. The people must base their unity on technical and rational grounds. The people need a team of leaders whose ideology is realistic and based on present-day Colombian circumstances. The leaders must be willing to sacrifice their personalities to fulfill a scientific ideal. They must be able to abandon the traditional and sentimental in favor of the technological. They must learn to put aside philosophic and normative principles, not as regards their personal lives and ultimate objectives, but insofar as such self-assertion would divide those who seek for concrete, scientific action in favor of the masses and of the country.

The leaders must be able to forego imported theoretical schemes and use their talents to find Colombian solutions to Colombián problems in order to effect a solid and definitive transformation of our institutions.

Camilo Torres

May, 1965

THE LAST PROCLAMATION OF CAMILO TORRES TO THE COLOMBIAN PEOPLE

From the mountains—January, 1966.

Colombians:

For many years the poor of our country have waited for the battle cry marking the final struggle against the oligarchy.

At those times when the despair of the people has reached an extreme the ruling class has always found a way of tricking the people, of distracting them and pacifying them with new formulas which always end up the same way: suffering for the people and comfort for the privileged class.

When the people cried for a leader and found him in Jorge Eliecer Gaitan, the oligarchy killed him. When the people begged for peace the oligarchy unleashed violence. When the people could no longer stand the violence and organized wars to take power the oligarchy contrived the military coup so that the betrayed guerrilla fighters would turn themselves in. When the people asked for democracy they were deceived again by a plebiscite and a National Front which meant dictatorship by the oligarchy.

125

Now the people will never believe again. They do not believe in elections. They know that legal means have been exhausted. They see force as the only means left. The people are desperate and ready to give their lives to save the next generation of Colombians from slavery. They want their children to have life, education, shelter, food, clothing and, above all, dignity. They want their children to live in an independent Colombia, free from the power of the United States.

All genuine revolutionaries must see force as the only means left. The people are waiting for the leaders to give the battle cry by their example and presence.

I want to tell the Colombian people that this is the moment, that I have not betrayed them; that I have walked through the streets and parks of our towns and cities in an effort to unite and organize the popular class for the take-over of power. I have asked that, if necessary, we even give up our lives for these objectives.

Now all is ready. The oligarchy wants to organize another farcical election, with candidates who resign and then accept again, with bipartisan committees, with movements for renewal which group not only old persons with old ideas, but persons who have betrayed the people. What else are we waiting for, Colombians?

I am joining the armed struggle. From the Colombian mountains I mean to continue the fight with a gun in my hand until power is won for the

126

people. I have joined the Army of National Liberation because I have found the desire for and the realization of unity at the base, the peasant base, without religious or traditional party differences, without antagonism toward the revolutionary principles of other sectors, movements or parties, without caudillism. The Army of National Liberation seeks to free the people from imperialism and from exploitation by the oligarchs and will not lay down its arms as long as power is not entirely in the hands of the people. Its accepted objectives are those of the United Front.

All patriotic Colombians must be ready for war. Little by little experienced guerrilla chiefs will arise throughout the country. In the meantime we must be alert. We must gather arms and ammunition and train in guerrilla fighting. We must talk with those who are thoroughly familiar with the situation. We must organize troops and collect drugs and provisions in preparation for a prolonged struggle.

Let us inflict small difficulties on the enemy where we are sure of victory. Let us test those who call themselves revolutionaries. Let us be rid of the traitors. Let us not cease activity, but neither let us be impatient. In a drawn-out war everyone, at some time, will have a chance to participate. What is important is that the revolution find us ready at all times. It is not necessary that we all be doing everything; we must distribute the work. The military men of the United Front must be in the vanguard of initiative and action. Let us be patient in the hope and confidence of final victory.

The struggle of the people must be a national struggle. We have already started because the journey will be long.

Colombians: Let us not be deaf to the call of the people and of the revolution!

Military men of the United Front: Let us make our watch-words a reality!

For the unity of the popular class until death!

For the organization of the popular class until death!

For the take-over of power by the popular class until death!

Until death because we are decided to fight until the end!

Until victory because a people which gives itself wholly to a cause achieves victory!

Until the final victory with the watch-words of the Army of National Liberation!

Not one step back . . . Liberty or death!

Camilo Torres